Soups & Sandwiches

Wholesome Ideas for Quick Lunches

SOUPS & SANDWICHES

WHOLESOME IDEAS FOR QUICK LUNCHES

CRESCENT BOOKS
New York/Avenel, New Jersey

This 1992 edition published by Crescent Books, distributed
by Outlet Book Company, Inc., a Random House Company,
40 Engelhard Avenue, Avenel, New Jersey 07001, USA

Printed and bound in Italy

CREDITS

Editor: Sue Felstead

Contributing authors: Lorna Rhodes and Louise Steele

Typeset by: BMD Graphics, Hemel Hempstead

Color separation by: Kentscan Ltd.

Contributing photographers: Paul Grater and
Jon Stewart, assisted by Kay Small

Contents

SOUPS

Introduction

Soups are not just for cold winter days as this collection shows. As you can see, there is an interesting range of chilled soups which would be perfect for an *'al fresco'* summer meal. Vichyssoise and Gazpacho are both familiar dishes, while the Summer Avocado Soup, lightly curried Senegalese Soup and the Iced Fennel Soup are unusual and tempting recipes. For a real conversation piece, try one of the fruit-based soups such as the delicious Finnish Berry Soup or the classic Soup Normande based on apples. Take a close look at the photographs as they demonstrate a wealth of garnishing ideas, some are very simple while others call more upon your creative skills – do mix and match the soups and finishes.

Stock is the most essential ingredient in many good soups. There are two basic kinds of soup, those which are blended and those which consist of chunky ingredients in a liquid base. With smooth soups, try using one of the many varieties of stock cube, such as additive-free vegetarian bouillon, or cubes based on onions or even bell peppers. Commercial stock is often quite salty, so use with care. Broth-based soups need a good stock base and the best of these are home-made. The only substitute that can be used is tinned (canned) consommé, which is a useful standby for emergencies. Dilute the consommé with a little water, vegetable cooking water, or vegetable juice.

To make home-made poultry stock, place a chicken or turkey carcass along with the giblets into a large saucepan. Cover with water along with 2 carrots, 2 sticks celery, bouquet garni and 1 teaspoon black peppercorns. Add salt to taste. Bring to the boil, skim off any residue which rises to the surface, cover and simmer for two hours. Check the water level from time to time to ensure that the bones are covered. Strain and leave the stock to cool. Discard any fat that rises to the surface. If you plan on freezing the stock, boil rapidly after straining until the liquid is reduced by half. Do not forget to dilute this concentrated mixture with water when you come to use the stock. For a white stock, use veal bones. For a beef stock, substitute beef marrow bone.

Vegetable stock can be made by keeping the boiling water from cooked vegetables and freezing it. To develop a fuller flavor, you may wish to add a large quartered onion, bouquet garni and peppercorns to the vegetable water, then simmer the stock for approximately 30 minutes. Vegetable extract is available in health food shops and improves the flavor of vegetable water. It is also useful for making quick vegetarian stocks.

When preparing soups, season carefully. As the liquid evaporates and the ingredients cook together, the liquids become more concentrated and mature so it is best to leave the seasoning until just before serving. Similarly with cold soups, check the seasoning once the soup is chilled to be sure that the balance of flavors is correct.

Most soups freeze well. Allow the cooked soup to cool, then place in a container leaving a space of 1 inch at the top. Seal and freeze. Thaw for several hours at room temperature, in either a saucepan over a low heat or on the thaw or low setting in the microwave. Soups that contain milk, cream or an egg-based thickening mixture should be frozen before these ingredients are added to prevent curdling. Fish soups and oriental soups should be eaten immediately after preparation as the flavors and texture will deteriorate and over heating will spoil the soup. Soups made with meat, on the other hand, often benefit from being refrigerated overnight as it gives flavors a chance to mature.

Many soups can be made in under half an hour, especially if canned ingredients and stock cubes are used. The Tomato & Rice Soup is based on tomatoes, and canned tomatoes are an excellent substitute for the fresh tomatoes specified. Mexican Bean Soup requires canned beans and sweetcorn. Soup that is made with seasonal ingredients is generally inexpensive.

Soup is a good choice of meal for children. As a rule, children do not like their food too spicy, so divide off their portion, before seasoning the remainder for the adults. Young babies in particular should avoid taking salted food. The best bet is to make a soup that is smooth in texture and red to orange in color. A good example is the mildly flavored Golden Vegetable Soup or Gazpacho, or why not purée some Tomato & Zucchini Soup. Many children will reject the idea of cold soup. Another good choice is a chicken-based soup, such as Rich Country Chicken or Chicken Noodle Soup.

FLORENTINE SOUP

AVGOLÉMONO

1-1/2 lbs. fresh spinach
1/4 cup butter
1 shallot, chopped
1/4 cup all-purpose flour
2-1/2 cups chicken or vegetable stock
Salt and pepper to taste
1/4 teaspoon grated nutmeg
2-1/2 cups milk
3 tablespoons whipping cream
1/4 cup whipping cream and 2 very small eggs, hard cooked, sliced, to garnish

Pick over spinach, discarding stalks, and wash thoroughly.

Cook spinach in a large saucepan over medium heat until tender. Pour spinach into a colander set over a bowl and press out as much water as possible. Melt butter in a large saucepan. Cook shallot in butter until soft. Blend in flour and cook 1 minute. Add spinach and stock and simmer 15 minutes. Season with salt and pepper. Add nutmeg.

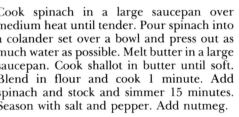

In a food processor fitted with a metal blade or a blender, process soup mixture to a puree. Clean pan and return puree to clean pan. Add milk and reheat gently. Just before serving, stir in 3 tablespoons whipping cream. To serve, swirl 1 tablespoon of whipping cream on each portion of soup and garnish with hard-cooked egg slices. Makes 4 servings.

5 cups chicken stock
Salt and pepper to taste
1/3 cup long-grain white rice
2 eggs
Finely grated peel 1/2 lemon
Juice 1 lemon
3 tablespoons chopped fresh parsley
Thin lemon slices and fresh flat-leaf parsley leaves to garnish

Bring stock to a boil in a large saucepan. Season with salt and pepper. Stir in rice, cover and simmer 15 minutes or until rice is tender.

In a small bowl, beat eggs and lemon peel and juice. Whisk a ladleful of hot stock into egg mixture, then pour mixture back into stock, stirring constantly.

Reheat over low heat until soup thickens and looks creamy. Do not allow to boil. Stir in chopped parsley. Garnish with lemon slices and parsley leaves and serve at once. Or serve soup cold, if desired. Makes 4 to 6 servings.

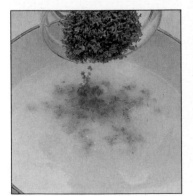

— CHILLED GREEN ONION SOUP —

— ICED FENNEL SOUP —

2 bunches green onions
1 tablespoon olive oil
3-3/4 cups vegetable stock
Salt and pepper to taste
1 hard-cooked egg

Trim green stems from green onions and set aside. Chop white parts. In a large saucepan, saute white parts in oil until soft.

2 medium-size fennel bulbs, (1 lb. total)
1 tablespoon sunflower oil
1 small onion, chopped
3 cups chicken or vegetable stock
2/3 cup dairy sour cream
Salt and pepper to taste

Remove green feathery leaves from fennel and reserve. Coarsely chop bulbs. Heat oil in a large saucepan over medium heat. Add fennel and onion. Cover and simmer 10 minutes.

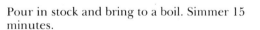

Pour in stock and bring to a boil. Simmer 15 minutes.

Add stock. Bring to a boil. Reduce heat and simmer about 20 minutes or until fennel is tender. Reserve several chopped fennel pieces for garnish.

Chop green onion stems and stir into soup. Cook 2 minutes, then cool soup. Chill and season with salt and pepper. Chop hard-cooked egg and stir into soup. Makes 4 servings.

In a food processor fitted with a metal blade or a blender, process soup to a puree. Cool, then whisk in sour cream. Season with salt and pepper. Chill and check seasoning again before serving. Garnish soup with reserved fennel pieces. Makes 6 servings.

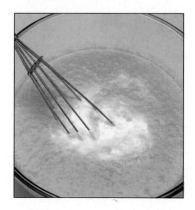

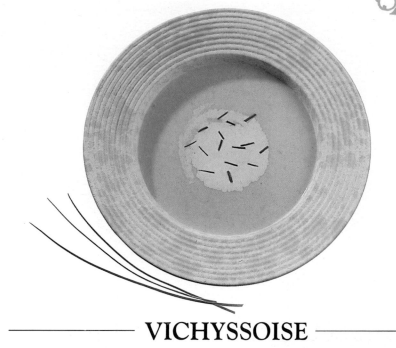

CHILLED FISH SOUP

1 lb. unpeeled cooked shrimp
3-3/4 cups water
2 strips lemon peel
2 bay leaves
2 blades mace
Salt and pepper to taste
4 small prepared squid, cleaned
Green stems 2 green onions, chopped
4 tomatoes, peeled, seeded, chopped
2 tablespoons peeled chopped cucumber

Peel shrimp and reserve. Place shells, head and tails in a large saucepan. Add water, lemon peel, bay leaves and mace. Season with salt and pepper.

Bring to a boil and simmer 30 minutes. Strain stock through a muslin-lined sieve or coffee filter paper set over a bowl. Return stock to pan. Cut squid in thin rings and chop tentacles. Cook squid in stock 5 minutes and cool.

Stir in reserved shrimp, green onions, tomatoes and cucumber. Season again if necessary. Refrigerate at least 1 hour before serving. Makes 4 servings.

VICHYSSOISE

2 tablespoons butter
3 medium-size leeks, trimmed, sliced, washed
1 shallot, finely chopped
8 ozs. potatoes, sliced
3 cups light chicken stock
Pinch ground mace or grated nutmeg
Salt and pepper to taste
2/3 cup half and half
Snipped chives to garnish

Melt butter in a large saucepan. Cook leeks and shallot in butter, covered, over low heat 10 minutes without browning. Add potatoes, stock and mace. Bring to a boil, cover and simmer 20 minutes.

In a food processor fitted with a metal blade or a blender, process mixture to a puree. Strain puree through a sieve set over a bowl. Season with salt and pepper.

Cool and stir in 2/3 of half and half. Refrigerate until ready to serve. Swirl in remaining half and half. Garnish soup with snipped chives. Makes 6 servings.

WINTER VEGETABLE SOUP — — CLEAR VEGETABLE SOUP —

2 tablespoons butter
1 medium-size onion, sliced
8 ozs. carrots, diced
8 ozs. rutabagas, diced
1 medium-size potato, diced
2 large parsnips, diced
2 cups vegetable stock
1 bay leaf
1 tablespoon cornstarch
2 cups milk
Salt and pepper to taste
1 cup frozen green peas
2 small bread rolls
1/2 cup shredded Cheddar cheese (2 oz.)

Melt butter in a large saucepan. Add onion, carrots, rutabagas, potato and parsnips. Cover and cook over low heat 10 minutes. Add stock and bay leaf and simmer 30 minutes. In a small bowl, blend cornstarch with a small amount of milk, then add to soup. Pour remaining milk into soup and heat, stirring until soup thickens. Remove bay leaf and season with salt and pepper.

Stir green peas into soup and simmer over low heat. Cut bread rolls in half. Sprinkle with cheese. Broil until cheese is melted. Serve bread rolls with soup. Makes 4 servings.

2 carrots, thinly sliced
2 stalks celery, sliced
2 ozs. button mushrooms, sliced
1-1/4 cups broccoli flowerets
1/2 cup frozen green peas
1 zucchini, cut in strips
Salt and pepper to taste
Fresh flat-leaf parsley sprigs to garnish

Vegetable Stock:
1 small onion, thinly sliced
1 leek, chopped
2 stalks celery, chopped
3 carrots, chopped
2 tomatoes, chopped
5 cups water
Bouquet garni
2 bay leaves
Salt to taste
1/2 teaspoon black peppercorns

To prepare stock, combine all stock ingredients in a large saucepan. Bring to a boil and simmer 40 minutes. For a stronger flavor, boil rapidly 5 minutes or until stock is reduced to 3-3/4 cups. Strain stock into a large bowl. Clean pan and return strained stock to clean pan. Add carrots, celery, mushrooms and broccoli. Bring to a boil. Cover and simmer 5 minutes.

Stir in green peas and zucchini and cook 2 minutes. Season with salt and pepper. Garnish with parsley sprigs. Makes 4 servings.

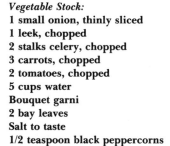

FRENCH ONION SOUP

FRENCH TURNIP SOUP

2 tablespoons butter
2 tablespoons olive oil
1 lb. onions, thinly sliced
Pinch sugar
5 cups beef stock
1 bay leaf
Salt and pepper to taste
4 thick slices French bread stick
1 teaspoon Dijon-style mustard
3/4 cup shredded Gruyère cheese (3 oz.)

Heat butter and oil in a large saucepan. Add onions and sugar.

2 tablespoons butter
1 lb. small white turnips
1 small onion, chopped
5 cups vegetable stock
4 slices white bread, crusts removed
4 ozs. shelled fresh green peas
Salt and pepper to taste
Pinch grated nutmeg

Cheese Puffs:
4 ozs. puff pastry
3 tablespoons cream cheese with herbs and
   garlic
1 egg, beaten

Heat butter in a large saucepan. Add turnips and onion.

Cook over medium heat about 20 minutes, stirring occasionally, until onions are a deep golden brown. Add stock and bay leaf and slowly bring to a boil. Simmer 25 minutes. Remove bay leaf and season with salt and pepper.

Cook gently 10 minutes or until they begin to soften. Add stock and bread and simmer gently 25 minutes. In a food processor fitted with a metal blade or a blender, process mixture to a puree. Clean pan and return puree to clean pan. Blanch peas in boiling salted water 2 minutes, then add peas to soup. Season with salt and pepper. Add nutmeg.

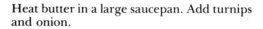

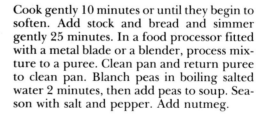

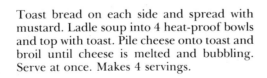

Toast bread on each side and spread with mustard. Ladle soup into 4 heat-proof bowls and top with toast. Pile cheese onto toast and broil until cheese is melted and bubbling. Serve at once. Makes 4 servings.

To prepare puffs, preheat oven to 400F (205C). Grease a baking sheet. Roll out pastry thinly and cut in 2-inch rounds. Place 1/2 teaspoon of cheese in center of each round. Dampen edge of pastry, then fold over and place on greased baking sheet. Bake in preheated oven until crisp and golden. Garnish soups with puffs. Makes 4 servings.

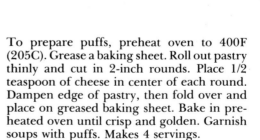

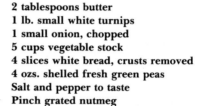

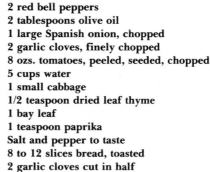

— HARVEST BARLEY SOUP —

1/3 cup pearl barley
5 cups vegetable stock
1 large carrot, diced
1 small turnip, diced
1 stalk celery, chopped
1 small onion, finely chopped
2 young leeks, sliced
1/2 teaspoon mixed dried herbs
1 tablespoon plus 2 teaspoons tomato paste
Salt and pepper to taste
1 bay leaf
1 (7-1/2-oz.) can butter beans, drained

Cheesey Croutons:
1 thick slice bread
1/2 cup shredded Cheddar cheese (2 oz.)

In a large saucepan, combine barley and stock. Bring to a boil and simmer 45 minutes or until barley is tender. Stir in prepared vegetables, herbs and tomato paste. Season with salt and pepper. Add bay leaf. Simmer 20 minutes. To prepare croutons, toast bread on both sides. Remove crusts and sprinkle bread with cheese. Broil until cheese is melted and golden.

Remove bay leaf and stir in beans. Gently cook 5 minutes to heat through. Cut croutons in squares and garnish soup. Makes 4 to 6 servings.

— MINORCAN VEGETABLE SOUP —

2 red bell peppers
2 tablespoons olive oil
1 large Spanish onion, chopped
2 garlic cloves, finely chopped
8 ozs. tomatoes, peeled, seeded, chopped
5 cups water
1 small cabbage
1/2 teaspoon dried leaf thyme
1 bay leaf
1 teaspoon paprika
Salt and pepper to taste
8 to 12 slices bread, toasted
2 garlic cloves cut in half

Broil bell peppers until skins are blisted and charred, turning over once.

Place in a plastic bag and let stand 15 minutes. Peel bell peppers, remove tops and seeds and chop. Heat oil in a large saucepan. Add onion and cook until soft. Add bell peppers, garlic and tomatoes. Cover pan and cook gently 15 minutes. Pour in water and bring to a boil.

Discard outer leaves of cabbage. Shread remaining cabbage. Add shredded cabbage, thyme, bay leaf and paprika to soup. Simmer 15 minutes. Season with salt and pepper. To serve, rub toast with a cut side of garlic. Place toast in soup bowls, then ladle hot soup over toast. Serve at once. Makes 4 to 6 servings.

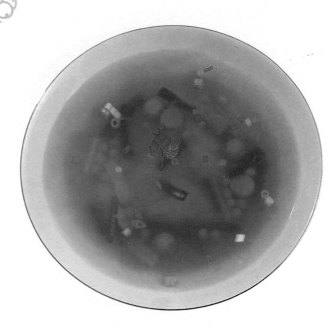

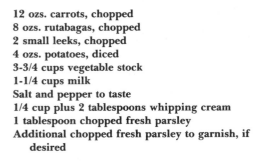

SUMMER VEGETABLE SOUP

2/3 cup tomato juice
2-1/2 cups vegetable stock
Grated peel and juice 1/2 lemon
2 large carrots
1/2 red bell pepper, seeded, cut in thin strips
1/2 yellow bell pepper, seeded, cut in thin
  strips
1 oz. freshly shelled green peas
4 green onions, sliced
Fresh chervil to garnish

In a large bowl, combine tomato juice and stock. Whisk in lemon peel and juice. Pour into a soup tureen and refrigerate until chilled.

Cut out tiny balls from carrot with a baller or dice. Blanch carrots, bell peppers and peas in boiling water 2 minutes. Refresh under cold water.

Stir blanched vegetables and green onions into soup. Garnish soup with chervil. Makes 4 servings.

GOLDEN VEGETABLE SOUP

12 ozs. carrots, chopped
8 ozs. rutabagas, chopped
2 small leeks, chopped
4 ozs. potatoes, diced
3-3/4 cups vegetable stock
1-1/4 cups milk
Salt and pepper to taste
1/4 cup plus 2 tablespoons whipping cream
1 tablespoon chopped fresh parsley
Additional chopped fresh parsley to garnish, if
  desired

In a large saucepan, combine all vegetables and stock. Bring to a boil. Cover and simmer 30 minutes.

In a food processor or a blender, process mixture to a puree. Clean pan and return puree to clean pan. Stir in milk. Reheat and season with salt and pepper.

In a small bowl, whip cream until soft peaks form. Fold in 1 tablespoon chopped parsley. Top portions of soup with herb chantilly. Garnish with additional chopped parsley, if desired. Makes 4 to 6 servings.

CARROT & CILANTRO SOUP

MINESTRONE

1 lb. carrots
2 tablespoons olive oil
1 small onion, finely chopped
1 garlic clove, crushed
1 teaspoon coriander seeds, crushed
1 teaspoon ground coriander
3-3/4 cups vegetable stock
Salt and pepper to taste
1/3 cup dark raisins, chopped
1 tablespoons chopped fresh cilantro

Sesame Croutons:
1 thick slice bread, crusts removed
1 tablespoon butter
1 tablespoon sesame seeds

2 tablespoons olive oil
1 medium-size onion, chopped
1 garlic clove, crushed
1 small leek, sliced
2 carrots, diced
2 stalks celery, sliced
7-1/2 cups chicken or beef stock
1 tablespoon tomato paste
1 (14-oz.) can navy beans, drained
3 tomatoes, peeled, seeded, chopped
2 ozs. green beans, cut in short lengths
2 cups shredded cabbage
1 oz. soup pasta
Salt and pepper to taste
2 tablespoons chopped fresh parsley
Freshly grated Parmesan cheese to garnish

Dice 2 carrots and set aside. Chop remaining carrots. Heat oil in a large saucepan. Gently cook chopped carrots, onion and garlic in oil 10 minutes. Stir in crushed coriander seeds and ground coriander and cook 1 minute. Pour in 3 cups of stock. Cover, bring to a simmer and cook 15 minutes or until carrots are tender. Meanwhile, in a small saucepan, simmer diced carrots in remaining stock until carrots are tender.

Heat oil in a large saucepan. Cook onion, garlic and leek over low heat 5 minutes. Stir in carrots, celery, stock, tomato paste and drained beans and bring to a simmer. Cover and cook 30 minutes. Stir in tomatoes and green beans and simmer 10 minutes.

In a food processor fitted with a metal blade or a blender, process mixture to a puree. Clean pan and return puree to clean pan. Stir cooked diced carrots with stock and raisins into puree. Season with salt and pepper. Reheat gently. To prepare croutons, toast bread on each side until golden. Cool, spread with butter and sprinkle with sesame seeds. Toast until golden. Cut toast in small cubes. Stir chopped cilantro into soup. Garnish soup with sesame seed croutons. Makes 4 servings.

Stir in cabbage and pasta. Season with salt and pepper. Cook 10 minutes or until pasta is tender. Stir in parsley. Garnish with cheese. Makes 6 servings.

COUNTRY MUSHROOM SOUP

GARLIC SOUP

1 medium-size onion, thinly sliced
1/3 cup brown rice
6 cups chicken stock
3 tablespoons butter
1 lb. fresh mushrooms, wiped clean, trimmed,
    sliced
1/4 cup plus 1 tablespoon dry sherry
Salt and pepper to taste
Fresh parsley sprigs to garnish

In a large saucepan, combine onion, brown rice and stock. Bring to a boil, then simmer 25 minutes.

3 tablespoons butter
6 garlic cloves
1/4 cup all-purpose flour
2-1/2 cups chicken stock
2/3 cup dry white wine
1 teaspoon dried leaf thyme
Salt and pepper to taste
1 egg yolk
2/3 cup half and half
3/4 cup ground almonds
Seedless green grapes, cut in half, to garnish

Melt butter in a large saucepan. Slightly crush garlic. Cook garlic in butter over low heat 3 to 4 minutes or until golden.

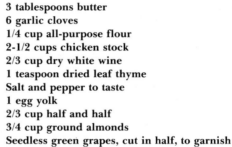

Meanwhile, melt butter in a large saucepan. Gently cook mushrooms about 10 minutes or until golden brown and most of moisture has evaporated.

Stir in flour, then gradually blend in stock. Stir in wine and thyme. Season with salt and pepper and simmer 10 minutes. In a large bowl, beat egg yolk and half and half . Strain stock mixture into bowl, whisking constantly.

Add mushrooms to stock. Stir in sherry and season with salt and pepper. Simmer 10 minutes. Garnish with parsley sprigs and serve hot. Makes 6 servings.

Variation: Use 2 or more varieties of mushrooms (button and open or chestnut mushrooms) which have a very good flavor. Wild mushrooms can be used if available.

Clean pan and return mixture to clean pan. Stir in almonds and reheat without boiling. Garnish soup with grapes. Makes 4 servings.

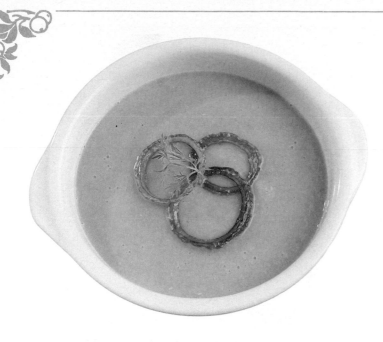

SPICY LENTIL SOUP

2 tablespoons olive oil
1/2 teaspoon cumin seeds
1 medium-size onion, chopped
1 garlic clove, crushed
2 carrots, chopped
2 stalks celery, chopped
1/2 teaspoon chili powder
1/2 teaspoon turmeric
1 teaspoon ground coriander
6 oz. red lentils, washed
5 cups vegetable stock
1 bay leaf
Salt and pepper to taste
Fried onion rings and fresh tarragon sprigs to
    garnish

Heat oil in a large saucepan over medium heat. Add cumin seeds. When seeds begin to pop, add onion and cook until golden. Add garlic, carrots and celery and cook gently 10 minutes. Stir in all spices and cook 1 minute, then add lentils.

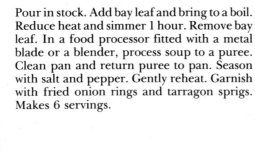

Pour in stock. Add bay leaf and bring to a boil. Reduce heat and simmer 1 hour. Remove bay leaf. In a food processor fitted with a metal blade or a blender, process soup to a puree. Clean pan and return puree to pan. Season with salt and pepper. Gently reheat. Garnish with fried onion rings and tarragon sprigs. Makes 6 servings.

SNOW PEA SOUP

2 tablespoons butter
5 green onions, chopped
12 ozs. Chinese snow peas, trimmed
2-1/2 cups chicken stock
1/2 small head lettuce, shredded
1 teaspoon sugar
Salt and pepper to taste
1 tablespoon chopped fresh mint
2/3 cup crème fraiche
2 slices bread
Oil for frying

Melt butter in a large saucepan. Gently cook green onions in butter 3 to 4 minutes.

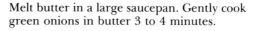

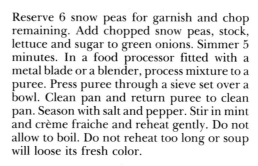

Reserve 6 snow peas for garnish and chop remaining. Add chopped snow peas, stock, lettuce and sugar to green onions. Simmer 5 minutes. In a food processor fitted with a metal blade or a blender, process mixture to a puree. Press puree through a sieve set over a bowl. Clean pan and return puree to clean pan. Season with salt and pepper. Stir in mint and crème fraiche and reheat gently. Do not allow to boil. Do not reheat too long or soup will loose its fresh color.

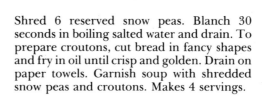

Shred 6 reserved snow peas. Blanch 30 seconds in boiling salted water and drain. To prepare croutons, cut bread in fancy shapes and fry in oil until crisp and golden. Drain on paper towels. Garnish soup with shredded snow peas and croutons. Makes 4 servings.

ZUCCHINI & TOMATO SOUP

GAZPACHO

2 tablespoons butter
1 medium-size onion, finely chopped
12 ozs. zucchini, coarsely grated
1 garlic clove, crushed
2-1/2 cups vegetable stock
1 (14-oz.) can chopped tomatoes
2 tablespoons chopped fresh mixed herbs, if
    desired
Salt and pepper to taste
1/4 cup whipping cream and fresh basil leaves
    to garnish

Melt butter in a large saucepan. Cook onion
in butter over medium heat until soft. Stir in
zucchini and garlic and cook 4 to 5 minutes.

Stir in stock and tomatoes with juice. Bring to
a boil and simmer 15 minutes.

Stir in herbs, if desired, and season with salt
and pepper. Garnish with dollops of
whipping cream and basil leaves. Makes 4
servings.

1 lb. ripe tomatoes, peeled, chopped
1/2 cucumber, peeled, chopped
1 green bell pepper, seeded, chopped
1 red bell pepper, seeded, chopped
1 small onion, chopped
1 garlic clove, chopped
1 cup bread crumbs
2 tablespoons olive oil
2 tablespoons red wine vinegar
2 cups tomato juice
1/2 teaspoon dried leaf marjoram
Salt and pepper to taste

Process all ingredients in a food processor
fitted with a metal blade or a blender. Process
in 2 batches if necessary.

Blend until smooth. Soup should be con-
sistency of half and half. If soup is too thick,
add a small amount of iced water. Spoon soup
into a bowl. Cover and refrigerate about 2
hours.

When soup is well chilled, season again with
salt and pepper, if necessary, and add a few
ice cubes. Makes 4 to 6 servings.

Note: Gazpacho is traditionally served with a
selection of garnishes passed separately.
These are added to individual portions as
desired. Serve chopped hard-cooked eggs,
chopped cucumber, chopped onion,
chopped green or black olives and diced
green bell pepper in separate small bowls.

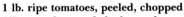

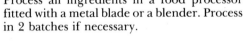

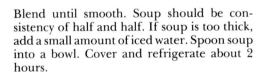

SURPRISE BEEF CONSOMMÉ

5 cups beef stock
8 ozs. lean ground beef
1 small onion, chopped
1 carrot, chopped
2 egg whites
Salt to taste
2 teaspoons Madeira wine or dry sherry
1 small truffle
12 ozs. puff pastry, thawed if frozen
1 egg, beaten

Remove any fat from stock. In a large saucepan, combine stock, ground beef and vegetables.

Whisk in egg whites. Bring slowly to a boil, whisking constantly. A thick gray scum will rise to surface. Reduce heat and simmer very gently, uncovered, 1 hour. Draw back scum and ladle clarified stock into a muslin-lined sieve set over a bowl. Consommé should be clear and sparkling. Season with salt and stir in wine. Ladle consommé into 6 individual ovenproof bowls. Cut truffle in small cubes and divide between bowls.

Preheat oven to 400F (205C). Roll out pastry and cut out 6 lids large enough to cover bowls, allowing enough to slightly overlap edge so pastry does not fall into soup. Brush top of pastry with beaten egg. Place bowls on a baking sheet. Bake in preheated oven 15 minutes or until pastry is risen and golden. Serve immediately. Makes 6 servings.

CREAMY CELERY & ONION SOUP

1 medium-size head celery
2 medium-size onions
1/4 cup butter
1 tablespoon all-purpose flour
3 cups milk
1 bay leaf
1/4 cup crème fraiche
Salt and pepper to taste

Cut 1 stalk of celery in thin strips. Place in a bowl of iced water and set aside. Reserve several celery leaves for garnish. Reserve 1/4 of 1 onion. Chop remaining onion and remaining celery.

Melt butter in a large saucepan. Cook chopped onion and celery in butter 5 minutes. Stir in flour, then gradually blend in milk. Add bay leaf, cover and simmer 20 minutes.

Cool soup slightly. Remove bay leaf. In a food processor fitted with a metal blade or a blender, process soup mixture to a puree. Clean pan and return puree to clean pan. Stir in crème fraiche. Season with salt and pepper, then reheat. Chop reserved onion and stir into soup. Drain celery curls. Garnish soup with celery curls and reserved celery leaves. Makes 4 to 6 servings.

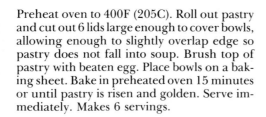

OMELETTE SOUP

5 cups chicken stock
3 eggs
1 tablespoons all-purpose flour
1/4 cup plus 2 tablespoons milk
Salt to taste
2 tablespoons freshly grated Parmesan cheese

In a large saucepan, bring stock to a boil. In a small bowl, beat eggs, flour, milk and salt.

Lightly grease bottom of a 7-inch skillet. Pour 1/3 of egg mixture into skillet. Cook until set and golden. Turn out onto a plate and roll up, jelly-roll style. Prepare 2 more omelettes.

Cut omelettes in thin strips. Add to stock. Reheat gently and sprinkle with grated cheese. Makes 4 servings.

CUCUMBER & YOGURT SOUP

1 large cucumber
1 small onion, chopped
1 tablespoon olive oil
2-1/2 cups hot chicken stock
Grated peel and juice 1/2 lemon
1 tablespoon chopped fresh dill
1/4 cup plus 2 tablespoons plain yogurt
Salt and pepper to taste
Fresh dill sprigs to garnish

Reserve 2 inches of cucumber, then chop remainder. In a large saucepan, saute onion in olive oil until soft. Add chopped cucumber, chicken stock, lemon peel and juice and chopped dill.

Bring to a boil, then cover and simmer 15 to 20 minutes. In a food processor fitted with a metal blade or a blender, process mixture to a puree. Pour into a bowl and cool. Stir in 1/2 of yogurt and refrigerate until chilled.

Season with salt and pepper. Thinly slice reserved piece of cucumber. To serve, float cucumber slices on soup and spoon remaining yogurt on top. Garnish with dill sprigs. Makes 4 to 6 servings

HOT & SOUR SOUP

5 cups chicken stock
3 tablespoons rice vinegar
1 tablespoon dry sherry
2 teaspoons soy sauce
1 small garlic clove, finely chopped
1/2 teaspoon finely chopped gingerroot
5 dried Chinese mushrooms, soaked in hot
    water 20 minutes
1 carrot, cut in thin strips
1 (3-oz.) can bamboo shoots, rinsed, cut in thin
    strips
1/2 teaspoon hot-pepper sauce or chili sauce
2 tablespoons cornstarch
3 tablespoons water
4 ozs. tofu, cut in strips
2 green onions, shredded

Bring stock to a boil in a large saucepan. Stir vinegar, sherry, soy sauce, garlic and gingerroot into stock. Remove stems from mushrooms and slice mushrooms. Add mushrooms, carrot, bamboo shoots and hot-pepper sauce to soup mixture. Bring to a boil, then simmer 10 minutes.

In a small bowl, blend cornstarch and water. Stir cornstarch and water and tofu into soup. Simmer 2 minutes or until thickened. Sprinkle with green onions. Makes 6 servings.

RED & YELLOW BELL PEPPER SOUP

1/4 cup butter
1 large onion, chopped
2 garlic cloves, crushed
8 ozs. tomatoes, coarsely chopped
8 ozs. red bell peppers, seeded, chopped
5 cups vegetable stock
8 ozs. yellow bell peppers, seeded, chopped
Salt and pepper to taste
1 tablespoon arrowroot
Water
1 oz. blanched almonds or pine nuts
1/2 slice white bread, crust removed
1/2 cup half and half

Place 1/2 of butter, 1/2 of onion and 1 garlic clove in a large saucepan.

Place remaining butter, onion and garlic in another large saucepan. Gently cook both until onion is soft. Add tomatoes, red bell peppers and 1/2 of stock to 1 pan. Add yellow bell peppers and remaining stock to other pan. Simmer both mixtures 20 minutes. In a food processor fitted with a metal blade or a blender, process 1 mixture to a puree. Press puree through a sieve set over a bowl. Clean pan and return puree to clean pan. Repeat procedure with remaining mixture. Season both purees with salt and pepper. In a small bowl, blend arrowroot with a small amount of water and stir into red bell pepper mixture. Reheat to thicken.

In food processor fitted with a metal blade or blender, process almonds, bread and half and half to a puree. Stir into yellow bell pepper puree and reheat. Pour each soup into a pitcher. Pour soups into individual bowls, pouring red bell pepper soup from 1 side and yellow bell pepper soup from opposite side. Serve at once. Makes 6 servings.

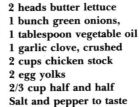

WATERCRESS & ALMOND SOUP

2 large bunches watercress
2 tablespoons butter
1 small onion
2 cups vegetable stock
1/3 cup blanched almonds, toasted, ground
1 tablespoon plus 1 teaspoon cornstarch
2 cups milk
Salt and pepper to taste
Flaked almonds, lightly toasted, to garnish

Wash watercress. Reserve a few sprigs to garnish. Cut away any coarse stalks and chop remainder.

Melt butter in a large saucepan. Saute onion in butter until soft. Add watercress. Cook 2 minutes, then stir in chicken stock. Cover and simmer 10 minutes.

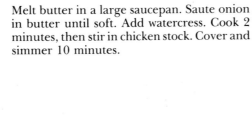

In a food processor fitted with a metal blade or a blender, process watercress mixture to a puree. Clean pan and return puree to pan. Stir in ground almonds. In a small bowl, blend cornstarch with a little milk. Add to watercress mixture, then stir in remaining milk. Simmer gently over low heat, stirring constantly, 5 minutes or until smooth. Remove from heat and cool. Refrigerate at least 4 hours or overnight. Garnish soup with flaked almonds and reserved watercress sprigs. Makes 4 servings.

LETTUCE SOUP

2 heads butter lettuce
1 bunch green onions,
1 tablespoon vegetable oil
1 garlic clove, crushed
2 cups chicken stock
2 egg yolks
2/3 cup half and half
Salt and pepper to taste

Trim lettuce, discarding any damaged leaves. Separate and wash leaves. Reserve a few for garnish, then shred remainder.

Heat oil in a large saucepan. Saute green onions and garlic in oil until tender. Add lettuce. Cover and cook until wilted. Pour in chicken stock and bring to a boil, then simmer 15 minutes. Pour through a sieve set over a bowl.

Return mixture to pan. In a small bowl, beat egg yolks and half and half. Stir into soup. Simmer over low heat until soup thickens. Do not allow to boil. Cool and refrigerate until chilled. To serve, roll up reserved lettuce leaves and finely slice. Stir into soup as a garnish. Makes 4 servings.

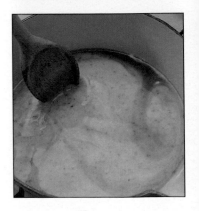

WATERCRESS CONSOMMÉ

HARLEQUIN CONSOMMÉ

Herb Pasta:
1 cup all-purpose flour
1 egg, beaten
1 teaspoon vegetable oil
2 teaspoons finely chopped fresh herbs
3 tablespoons water

Consommé:
3-3/4 cups beef consommé
2 small carrots, peeled, sliced, cut in flowers
12 watercress sprigs
3 tablespoons Madeira wine
Salt and pepper to taste

To prepare pasta, place flour in a medium-size bowl. Make a well in center and add egg, oil, herbs and water.

Mix until dough is soft and pliable. Turn onto a floured surface and knead until smooth. Wrap dough and let stand 30 minutes. Roll dough out thinly. Cover with a cloth and let dry 30 minutes, turning over after 15 minutes. Meanwhile, in a large saucepan, combine consommé, carrot and watercress stalks. Simmer 8 minutes.

Cut out small fancy shapes from pasta. Drop into boiling salted water and cook about 8 minutes or until tender. Remove watercress stalks from soup. Stir in watercress leaves and wine. Season with salt and pepper. Add pasta to consommé. Serve hot. Makes 4 to 6 servings.

1 lb. very lean ground beef
1 carrot, coarsely chopped
2 leeks, coarsely chopped
1/2 large red bell pepper, chopped
1/4 cup plus 1 tablespoon tomato paste
2 egg whites
5 cups beef stock
White of 1 hard-cooked egg
1/2 red bell pepper
Green leek leaves, blanched
1 carrot
Salt and pepper to taste

To prepare consommé, combine ground beef, chopped vegetables, tomato paste, egg whites and stock. Bring to a boil, whisking constantly. Reduce to a low simmer and cook 1-1/2 hours without stirring. Meanwhile, slice hard-cooked egg white and cut in small fancy shapes with aspic cutters. Cut shapes out of bell pepper and green leek leaves. Slice carrot thinly lengthwise, discarding core. Cut shapes from carrot strips.

Strain consommé through a muslin-lined sieve set over a bowl. Clean pan and return consommé to clean pan. Season with salt and pepper. Add bell pepper, leek and carrot shapes. Cook 1 minute, then add egg white shapes. Makes 6 servings.

BLACK BEAN SOUP

ITALIAN BEAN & PASTA SOUP

8 ozs. black beans
1 medium-size onion, finely chopped
2 tablespoons vegetable oil
1 bay leaf
5 cups water
5 cups vegetable or chicken stock
1 green or yellow bell pepper, seeded, diced
2 garlic cloves, crushed
1/3 cup brown rice
Salt and pepper to taste
4 ozs. ham, diced

Wash and pick over beans. Place beans in a large saucepan and cover with water.

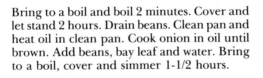

Bring to a boil and boil 2 minutes. Cover and let stand 2 hours. Drain beans. Clean pan and heat oil in clean pan. Cook onion in oil until brown. Add beans, bay leaf and water. Bring to a boil, cover and simmer 1-1/2 hours.

2 tablespoons olive oil
1 medium-size onion, finely chopped
1 garlic clove, crushed
2 celery stalks finely sliced
1 carrot, finely diced
1 tablespoon tomato paste
5 cups beef stock
1 (15-oz.) can red kidney beans, drained
3 ozs. small pasta shapes
4 ozs. frozen green peas
Salt and pepper to taste

Heat oil in a large saucepan. Add onion, garlic, celery and carrot. Stir and cook gently 5 minutes.

Add tomato paste, stock and beans. Bring to a boil and simmer 10 minutes.

Drain beans, onion and bay leaf. Clean pan and return beans, onion and bay leaf to clean pan. Stir in stock, bell pepper, garlic and rice. Season with salt and pepper. Simmer 1 hour or until beans are tender. Stir in diced ham and season again, if desired. Remove bay leaf. Makes 4 to 6 servings.

Add pasta and peas and cook another 7 minutes or until pasta is just cooked. Season with salt and pepper. Makes 4 to 6 servings.

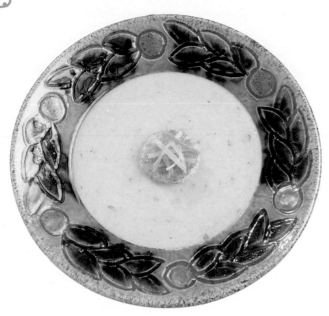

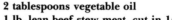

POTAGE BONNE FEMME

1/4 cup butter
1 lb. potatoes, diced
2 carrots, chopped
2 large leeks, chopped
7-1/2 cups vegetable stock
Salt and pepper to taste
1/2 cup whipping cream
1 tablespoon finely chopped fresh parsley or
    chervil
1/2 carrot, cut in fine strips, 1/2 small leek, cut
    in fine strips and 1 slice bread, toasted, to
    garnish

Melt butter in a large saucepan. Add prepared vegetables.

Cover and cook gently 15 minutes. Add stock, bring to a boil and simmer 20 minutes. In a food processor fitted with a metal blade or a blender, process mixture to a puree. Pass through a seive set over a bowl. Clean pan and return puree to clean pan. Season with salt and pepper. Stir in whipping cream and parsley and reheat very slowly.

To prepare garnish, blanch carrot and leek strips in boiling salted water 1 minute, then drain. Cut out 4 small rounds from toast. Top toast rounds with blanched vegetables. Garnish soup with blanched vegetables and toast rounds. Makes 4 servings.

GOULASH SOUP

2 tablespoons vegetable oil
1 lb. lean beef stew meat, cut in 1/4-inch cubes
1 large onion, thinly sliced
1 garlic clove, crushed
1/2 teaspoon ground cumin
2 teaspoons paprika
1 tablespoon all-purpose flour
5 cups beef stock
1 large potato
1 (14-oz.) can tomatoes, chopped, with juice
Salt and pepper to taste
Sour cream and paprika to garnish

Heat oil in a large saucepan and add beef and onion.

Cook over medium heat 4 minutes or until beef is brown and onion is soft. Stir in garlic, cumin, paprika and flour and cook 1 minute. Gradually add stock. Bring to a boil, then simmer 2 hours.

Dice potatoes. Add potatoes and tomatoes with juice to soup. Season with salt and pepper. Cook 30 minutes or until potatoes are tender. Garnish soup with sour cream and sprinkle with paprika. Makes 6 servings.

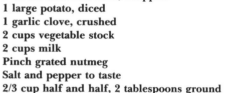

— CREAM OF MUSHROOM SOUP —

1/4 cup butter
12 ozs. mushrooms, finely chopped
1/2 cup all-purpose flour
2 cups chicken stock
2/3 cup milk
1 tablespoon chopped fresh parsley
1 tablespoon lemon juice
Salt and pepper to taste
2/3 cup half and half
1/4 cup plus 1 tablespoon whipping cream
1 tablespoon finely chopped watercress
Watercress leaves to garnish

Melt butter in a large saucepan. Gently cook mushrooms in butter 5 minutes.

Stir in flour, then gradually add stock and milk. Bring to a boil, then simmer 10 minutes. Add parsley and lemon juice. Season with salt and pepper. Stir in half and half and reheat gently.

In a small bowl, whip cream until soft peaks form. Stir in chopped watercress. Top each portion of soup with watercress chantilly. Garnish with watercress leaves. Makes 4 servings.

— CREAM OF BROCCOLI SOUP —

2 tablespoons butter
2 shallots, finely chopped
1 lb. broccoli flowerets, chopped
1 large potato, diced
1 garlic clove, crushed
2 cups vegetable stock
2 cups milk
Pinch grated nutmeg
Salt and pepper to taste
2/3 cup half and half, 2 tablespoons ground almonds and 1/4 teaspoon powdered saffron to garnish

Melt butter in a large saucepan. Cook shallots in butter 2 to 3 minutes or until soft. Add broccoli, potato and garlic. Cover and cook gently 5 minutes. Add stock and bring to a boil, then simmer 20 minutes or until vegetables are tender. In a food processor fitted with a metal blade or a blender, process mixture to a puree. Clean pan and return puree to clean pan. Add milk and nutmeg. Season with salt and pepper and reheat gently.

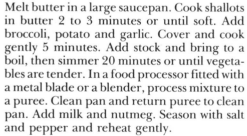

Divide half and half between 2 small bowls. Mix ground almonds into 1 bowl and saffron into other. Ladle soup into individual bowls. Garnish soup with alternate swirls of half and half mixtures. Makes 4 servings.

CREAM OF CAULIFLOWER SOUP

1 large cauliflower
1/4 cup butter
1 medium-size onion, chopped
1/4 cup all-purpose flour
2 cups chicken stock
2 cups milk
Salt and pepper to taste
Pinch grated nutmeg
1/4 cup crème fraiche

Cheese Snippets:
2 tablespoons grated Parmesan cheese
3 tablespoons butter
2 medium-size slices bread

Break cauliflower in flowerets.

Blanch cauliflower in boiling salted water 3 minutes, then drain. Melt butter in a large saucepan. Cook onion in butter until soft. Stir in flour, then gradually stir in stock. Bring to a boil and simmer 20 minutes. Strain into another large saucepan. Stir in milk and add cauliflower. Season with salt and pepper. Add nutmeg and simmer 10 minutes. Using a slotted spoon, reserve 1/3 of cauliflower.

In a food processor fitted with a metal blade or a blender, process mixture to a puree. Clean pan and return puree to clean pan. Stir in crème fraiche and reserved cauliflower. Reheat very slowly. Meanwhile to prepare snippets, preheat oven to 400F (205C). Beat cheese and butter in a small bowl. Spread butter-cheese over bread. Remove crusts, then cut in small squares or diamonds. Place on a baking sheet and bake in preheated oven until golden and crisp. Garnish soup with snippets. Makes 6 servings.

CREAM OF CARROT SOUP

2 tablespoons butter
1 small onion, finely chopped
1 medium-size potato, diced
1 lb. carrots, chopped
3 cups vegetable stock
Pinch sugar
2/3 cup half and half
Salt and pepper to taste

Herb Croutons:
2 tablespoons butter
1 teaspoon dried leaf herbs
2 slices bread

Melt butter in a large saucepan. Add onion, potato and carrots.

Cover and cook over low heat 10 minutes. Add stock and sugar. Bring to a boil, then simmer 30 minutes. In a food processor fitted with a metal blade or a blender, process mixture to a puree. Clean pan and return puree to clean pan. Stir in half and half and season with salt and pepper.

To prepare croutons, preheat oven to 400F (205C). Beat butter and herbs in a small bowl. Spread herbed butter over bread. Cut in fancy shapes or squares and place on a baking sheet. Bake in preheated oven until crisp and golden. Garnish soup with croutons. Makes 4 servings.

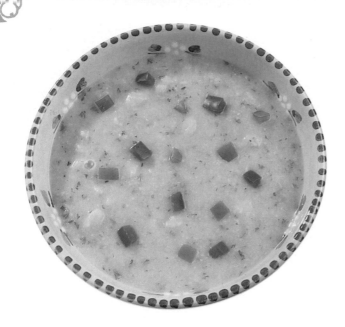

WHITE BEAN SOUP

MEXICAN BEAN SOUP

8 ozs. navy or cannellini beans,
   soaked overnight
3-3/4 cups chicken stock
3-3/4 cups water
Salt and pepper to taste
2 tablespoons olive oil
1 garlic clove, crushed
2 tablespoons chopped fresh parsley
1 tablespoon diced red bell pepper and 1
   tablespoon diced green bell pepper to
   garnish
Additional olive oil, if desired

Drain beans. In a large saucepan, combine
drained beans, stock and water.

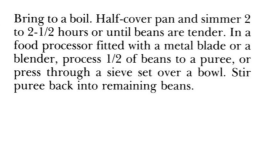

Bring to a boil. Half-cover pan and simmer 2
to 2-1/2 hours or until beans are tender. In a
food processor fitted with a metal blade or a
blender, process 1/2 of beans to a puree, or
press through a sieve set over a bowl. Stir
puree back into remaining beans.

2 tablespoons olive oil
1 medium-size onion, chopped
1 garlic clove, crushed
1 green bell pepper, seeded, diced
12 oz. ripe tomatoes, peeled, chopped
1/2 teaspoon chili powder
3-3/4 cups vegetable stock
2 tablespoons tomato paste
1 (15-oz.) can red kidney beans, drained
Salt and pepper to taste
1 avocado
1 cup whole kernel corn
Few drops hot-pepper sauce
1 tablespoon chopped fresh cilantro
Fresh cilantro sprigs to garnish

Heat oil in a large saucepan. Cook onion until
soft. Stir in garlic, bell pepper, tomatoes and
chili powder. Cook 3 to 4 minutes. Pour in
stock. Add tomato paste and 3/4 of beans.
Simmer 30 minutes. Cool slightly. In a food
processor fitted with a metal blade or a blender, process mixture to a puree.

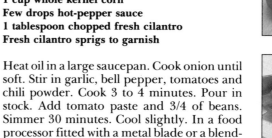

Heat oil in a small saucepan. Gently cook
garlic until soft. Do not allow to brown. Stir
garlic and parsley into soup and reheat slowly. Meanwhile, blanch diced bell peppers in
boiling water 2 minutes and drain. Garnish
soup with bell peppers. If desired, pour additional oil over soup. Makes 4 to 6 servings.

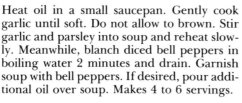
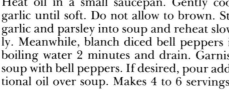

Clean pan and return puree to clean pan.
Season with salt and pepper. Cut avocado in
half. Remove seed, peel and dice. Stir
remaining beans, avocado, corn and
hot-pepper sauce into puree. Gently reheat
soup. Stir in chopped cilantro. Garnish with
cilantro sprigs. Makes 4 to 5 servings.

OXTAIL SOUP

1 oxtail, cut in pieces
3 tablespoons vegetable oil
2 stalks celery, chopped
2 carrots, chopped
2 small onions, sliced
6 cups water
2/3 cup red wine
Bouquet garni
6 black peppercorns, slightly crushed
1/2 teaspoon dried leaf thyme
4 whole cloves
Salt and pepper to taste
1/4 teaspoon cayenne pepper
1 tablespoon plus 1 teaspoon arrowroot

Parsley Dumplings:
1 recipe Watercress Dumplings, page 39
   (substitute 2 tablespoons chopped fresh
   parsley for watercress)

Wash oxtail and trim off any fat. Heat oil in a large saucepan. Add oxtail and fry until brown. Remove oxtail and cook vegetables in oil until they begin to brown. Add oxtail, water, wine, bouquet garni, peppercorns, thyme and cloves. Season with salt and pepper. Bring to a boil, skimming off any scum. Cover and simmer over very low heat 3 hours. Remove oxtail and cool. Remove meat from bones, discarding gristle. Strain soups through a sieve set over a bowl. Add oxtail meat to stock.

Prepare dumplings. Begin to reheat soup. In a small bowl, blend arrowroot with a small amount of water. Stir arrowroot and cayenne pepper into soup. Season again with salt and pepper, if necessary. When soup simmers, drop in dumplings. Cover and cook 20 minutes or until dumplings are done. Makes 6 servings.

PLOUGHMAN'S SOUP

3 tablespoons butter
2 medium-size onions, chopped
1/4 cup whole-wheat flour
2 cups chicken stock
1 cup light ale
Dash Worcestershire sauce
1-1/2 cups crumbled Cheshire cheese (6 oz.)
Salt and pepper to taste
Mild raw onion rings to garnish

Melt butter in a large saucepan. Gently cook onion until soft. Stir in whole-wheat flour and cook 1 minute.

Remove from heat and gradually blend in stock and ale. Return to heat and bring to a boil. Simmer 5 minutes or until thickened. Stir in Worcestershire sauce.

Reserve 1/4 cup cheese. Stir in remaining cheese, a little at a time, over a low heat until cheese is melted. Season with salt and pepper. Garnish with reserved cheese and onion rings. Makes 4 servings.

BEEF & PASTA SOUP

6 ozs. capellini (very fine spaghetti)

Beef Stock:
1 lb. boneless beef stew meat, cut in pieces
1 lb. marrow bones or knuckle of veal
7-1/2 cups water
1 medium-size onion, sliced
1 large carrot, sliced
Bouquet garni
1 teaspoon salt
5 peppercorns
1 bay leaf

Parmesan Balls:
1/4 cup freshly grated Parmesan cheese
2 egg yolks

Preheat oven to 425F (220C). In a large roasting pan, bake meat and bones in preheated oven 15 minutes or until brown. Turn meat and bones over and bake another 10 minutes. Transfer meat to a large saucepan. Add water and bring to a boil. Skim off scum which rises to surface. When only white foam is left, add onion, carrot, bouquet garni, salt, peppercorns and bay leaf. Simmer very gently 3 hours. This should yield 5 cups stock.

Strain stock, cool and refrigerate overnight. Next day, remove fat from surface of stock and return to a large saucepan. Reheat stock, seasoning again with salt and pepper, if necessary. When soup simmers, break up pasta and drop into soup. Cook 6 minutes. Meanwhile, to prepare Parmesan balls, mix cheese and egg yolks in a small bowl. Drop 1/2 teaspoonfuls of mixture over surface of soup. Cook about 4 minutes or until balls and pasta are done. Serve at once. Makes 6 servings.

MULLIGATAWNY

1 lb. boneless beef stew meat, cut in pieces
7-1/2 cups water
1 (2-inch) piece gingerroot, peeled
2 bay leaves
1 medium-size onion, chopped
1 teaspoon turmeric
1/2 teaspoon chili powder
2 teaspoons coriander seeds, crushed
2 teaspoons cumin seeds, crushed
8 black peppercorns, crushed
1 small cooking apple, peeled, cored, chopped
1 carrot, sliced
2 tablespoons red lentils
2 garlic cloves, chopped
Salt to taste
1 tablespoon lemon juice

Garlic Croutons:
2 thick slices bread
1/4 cup plus 2 tablespoons vegetable oil
3 garlic cloves, crushed

In a large saucepan, cover beef with water. Bring to a boil. Skim surface and add remaining ingredients except lemon juice. Simmer very gently 2-1/2 to 3 hours or until beef is tender. Meanwhile, to prepare croutons, cut off crusts from bread and dice bread. Heat oil in a medium-size skillet. Fry diced bread and garlic, turning bread constantly until crisp and golden. Remove with a slotted spoon and drain on a paper towel.

Remove beef and set aside. Pour stock through a sieve set over a bowl, rubbing vegetables through. Discard pulp. Cool, then refrigerate meat and stock until chilled. Remove solidified fat from surface of soup. Pour into a pan and reheat. Cut beef in small pieces. Add beef and lemon juice to soup and season again with salt, if necessary. Simmer 5 minutes. Garnish soup with croutons. Makes 4 to 6 servings.

GERMAN SAUSAGE SOUP

 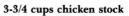

1 large potato, diced
1 large onion, sliced
3 stalks celery, chopped
1 (14-oz.) can chopped tomatoes
3-3/4 cups beef or ham stock
1/2 teaspoon caraway seeds
1 (8-oz.) can red kidney beans, drained
1 cup shredded cabbage
4 ozs. frankfurters, thickly sliced
1 (4 oz.) piece German sausage (bierwurst or
    ham sausage), diced
Salt and pepper to taste
Toast triangles, if desired

In a large saucepan, combine potato, onion, celery, tomatoes with juice, stock and caraway seeds.

Bring to a boil and simmer 20 minutes. Add drained beans and cabbage and simmer 20 minutes.

Stir in frankfurters and diced sausage. Season with salt and pepper and cook until heated through. Serve with toast triangles, if desired. Makes 4 to 6 servings.

CRAB & CORN SOUP

3-3/4 cups chicken stock
1 small piece gingerroot, peeled
2 teaspoons light soy sauce
1 tablespoon dry sherry
1 (15-oz.) can creamed corn
Salt and pepper to taste
2 teaspoons cornstarch
2 tablespoons water
4 ozs. crabmeat
2 eggs, beaten
2 green onions, finely sliced, to garnish

In a large saucepan, combine stock and gingerroot. Simmer 15 minutes. Remove gingerroot and stir in soy sauce, sherry and creamed corn. Season with salt and pepper. Simmer 5 minutes.

In a small bowl, blend cornstarch and water. Stir into stock mixture. Stir in crabmeat and heat until mixture thickens.

Bring mixture to a slow simmer and slowly pour in beaten eggs in a thin stream, stirring constantly. Do not allow soup to boil. Garnish soup with sliced green onions. Makes 4 to 6 servings.

TUNA & CORN BISQUE

SCALLOP & ARTICHOKE SOUP

2 tablespoons butter
1 small onion, finely chopped
1 teaspoon mild curry powder
1 teaspoon paprika
1/4 cup all-purpose flour
2 cups chicken stock
2 cups milk
Grated peel 1/2 lemon
1 (12-oz.) can whole kernel corn, drained
1 (7-oz.) can tuna, drained
1 tablespoon chopped fresh parsley and 1/2 cup shredded Cheddar cheese (2 ozs.) to garnish

Melt butter in a large saucepan and gently cook onion in butter until soft.

Stir in curry powder, paprika and flour and cook 1 minute. Gradually add stock and bring to a boil, stirring constantly. Stir in milk, lemon peel and corn and simmer 5 minutes.

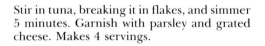

Stir in tuna, breaking it in flakes, and simmer 5 minutes. Garnish with parsley and grated cheese. Makes 4 servings.

1-1/4 lbs. Jerusalem artichokes
1 tablespoon lemon juice
1/4 cup butter
1 small onion, chopped
1 medium-size potato, diced
2-1/2 cups chicken stock
6 medium-size scallops
1-1/4 cups milk
Salt and pepper to taste
1/4 cup whipping cream
Chervil sprigs to garnish

Peel and slice artichokes. Stir lemon juice into a bowl of water. Place artichokes in lemon water.

Melt 3/4 of butter in a large saucepan. Drain artichokes. Gently cook artichokes and onion, covered, 10 minutes. Add potato and stock and bring to a boil. Simmer 15 to 20 minutes or until artichokes are soft. In a food processor fitted with a metal blade or a blender, process mixture to a puree. Clean pan and return puree to pan.

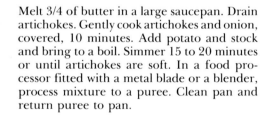

Cut white parts of scallops in small pieces, reserving corals. Stir scallops and milk into soup. Simmer a few minutes and season with salt and pepper. Melt remaining butter in a small skillet. Gently saute reserved scallop corals until firm. Slice corals in half. Stir whipping cream into soup and heat gently. Garnish soup with corals and chervil sprigs. Makes 4 servings.

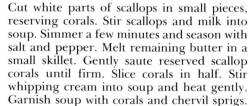

CREAMY FISH SOUP

Stock:
1 lb. fish heads, bones and trimmings
5 cups water
1 small onion, quartered
1 carrot, sliced
1 stalk celery, chopped
Bouquet garni
Salt to taste
6 black peppercorns
1 bay leaf
Lemon slice

Soup:
12 ozs. white fish fillets, skinned
3 tablespoons butter
1/3 cup all-purpose flour
2/3 cup half and half
Salt and pepper to taste
Lemon slices, chopped fresh dill or chervil
    sprigs and paprika to garnish

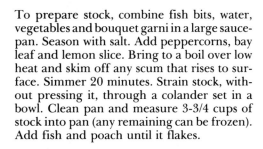

To prepare stock, combine fish bits, water, vegetables and bouquet garni in a large saucepan. Season with salt. Add peppercorns, bay leaf and lemon slice. Bring to a boil over low heat and skim off any scum that rises to surface. Simmer 20 minutes. Strain stock, without pressing it, through a colander set in a bowl. Clean pan and measure 3-3/4 cups of stock into pan (any remaining can be frozen). Add fish and poach until it flakes.

In a food processor fitted with a metal blade or a blender, process fish and a small amount of stock to a puree. Clean pan and melt butter in pan. Stir in flour and cook 1 minute without browning. Gradually add remainder of stock, then stir until boiling. Simmer 10 minutes. Whisk in fish puree and half and half. Season with salt and pepper. Garnish with lemon slices, chopped dill and paprika. Makes 4 to 6 servings.

CREAM OF SHRIMP SOUP

1 lb. unpeeled shrimp
1/4 cup butter
1 small onion, chopped
1/3 cup all-purpose flour
3 tablespoons dry white wine
2/3 cup half and half

Stock:
8 ozs. fish scraps and bones
1 strip lemon peel
1 stalk celery, chopped
1 small onion, quartered
5 fennel seeds
4 cups water
Salt and pepper to taste

Peel shrimp and reserve. In a large saucepan, combine shrimp shells with all stock ingredients. Slowly bring to a boil and remove any scum which rises to surface. Reduce heat and simmer 25 minutes. Strain through a muslin-lined sieve set over a bowl. Clean pan and return stock to clean pan. Simmer until stock is reduced to 3 cups.

Melt butter in saucepan. Gently cook onion in butter until soft. Stir in flour, then gradually blend in stock. Stir in wine and 3/4 of shrimp. Bring to a boil, then simmer 10 minutes. Cool soup slightly. In a food processor fitted with a metal blade or a blender, process soup to a puree. Clean pan and return puree to pan. Stir in half and half. Season with salt and pepper. Gently reheat 3 to 4 minutes. Garnish soup with reserved shrimp. Makes 4 servings.

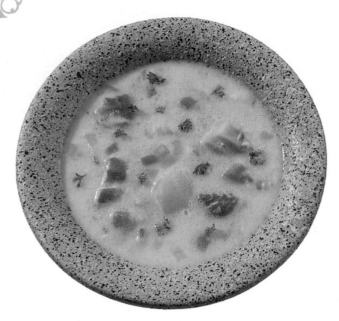

SMOKED HADDOCK CHOWDER

BOUILLABAISSE

1 lb. smoked haddock fillets, skinned
2 tablespoons butter
1 medium-size onion, chopped
2 cups fish stock
8 ozs. potatoes, diced
1 carrot, diced
1 bay leaf
1 tablespoon plus 1 teaspoon cornstarch
2 cups milk
1 cup fresh white bread crumbs
Squeeze lemon juice
Pepper to taste
Chopped fresh parsley to garnish

Cut fish in 1-inch pieces.

Melt butter in a large saucepan. Cook onion in butter over low heat until soft. Add stock, potato, carrot and bay leaf. Cover and simmer 15 minutes or until potatoes are just tender.

2 lbs. mixed fish (monkfish, cod, squid, mullet)
1 lb. shellfish (shrimp, mussels, scallops)
6 cups water
1 medium-size onion, sliced
1 carrot, sliced
1 stalk celery, chopped
1 bay leaf
Salt and pepper to taste
2 tablespoons olive oil
2 garlic cloves, finely chopped
2 small leeks, trimmed, finely chopped
4 tomatoes, peeled, chopped
Fresh fennel sprigs
3 orange peel strips
Good pinch saffron threads
1 fresh thyme sprig
Salt and pepper to taste
French bread, sliced, toasted
1 recipe Rouille, page 36

Clean and prepare fish, removing skin and bones. Reserve fish trimmings. Cut fish in chunks. Shellfish can be left unpeeled. Remove heads, if desired. In a large saucepan, combine fish trimmings and bones, water, onion, carrot, celery and bay leaf. Bring to a boil. Season with salt and pepper. Remove any scum which rises to surface and simmer 30 minutes. Strain stock into a large bowl, discarding bones and vegetables.

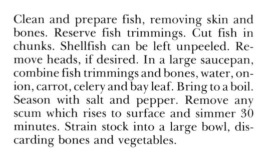

In a small bowl, blend cornstarch with a small amount of milk. Stir into soup with remaining milk and fish. Simmer gently 8 to 10 minutes or until fish is done. Do not allow to boil or fish will disintegrate. Remove bay leaf. Stir in bread crumbs and lemon juice. Season with pepper. Sprinkle with parsley. Makes 6 servings.

Clean saucepan. Heat oil in clean pan. Cook garlic and leeks over low heat 5 minutes. Add tomatoes and cook 5 minutes. Pour in stock and bring to a boil. Stir in fennel, orange peel, saffron and thyme. When mixture boils, reduce heat and add firmer white fish and simmer 8 minutes. Add shellfish and cook 5 minutes. Season with salt and pepper. Spread toast with Rouille and serve with soup. Makes 6 servings.

CARIBBEAN FISH SOUP

12 ozs. fresh tuna or swordfish steaks
Juice 1 lime
1 green chili pepper, seeded, finely chopped
2 garlic cloves, crushed
2 tablespoons sunflower oil
1 small onion, finely chopped
1 green bell pepper, seeded, diced
1 red bell pepper, seeded, diced
2/3 cup dry white wine
3 cups fish stock
1 teaspoon light-brown sugar
2 tomatoes, peeled, diced
1 small ripe mango, peeled, diced
Salt and pepper to taste

Cut fish in 1-inch pieces and place in a glass dish. Pour over lime juice and stir in chili pepper and garlic. Cover and refrigerate 1 hour. Heat oil in a large saucepan. Cook onion and bell peppers 5 minutes over medium heat. Stir in wine, stock and brown sugar and simmer 15 minutes.

Stir in tomatoes, mango and fish with marinade. Simmer gently 10 minutes. Season with salt and pepper and serve hot. Makes 4 to 6 servings.

SHRIMP BISQUE

8 ozs. unpeeled shrimp
1/4 cup butter
1 small onion, finely chopped
2/3 cup dry white wine
3-3/4 cups water
1 fish stock cube
1 bay leaf
Fresh parsley sprigs
3 strips lemon peel
1 tablespoon tomato paste
Salt and pepper to taste
1/4 cup all-purpose flour
Grated nutmeg
2/3 cup half and half

Peel a few shrimp and reserve for garnish.

Process remaining shrimp in a food processor fitted with a metal blade or a blender until finely chopped. Melt 1/2 of butter in a large saucepan. Gently cook onion in butter until soft. Stir in chopped shrimp and cook 4 to 5 minutes. Pour in wine and boil 2 minutes. Add water, stock cube, bay leaf, parsley, lemon peel and tomato paste. Season with salt and pepper and bring to a boil. Simmer, uncovered, 30 minutes, skimming off any froth that forms on surface. Pour mixture through a sieve set over a bowl. Discard bay leaf and parsley. In a food processor fitted with a metal blade or a blender, process solids in sieve and a small amount of liquid to a puree.

Clean sieve and pour puree through sieve into liquid. Clean pan and melt remaining butter. Stir in flour and cook 1 minute. Gradually blend in liquid. Stir in nutmeg and season with salt and pepper. Bring to a boil, stirring constantly. Simmer 3 minutes. Stir in 1/2 of half and half. Swirl remaining half and half on top of soup. Garnish with reserved shrimp. Makes 4 servings.

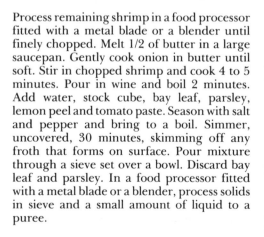

SOUPE DE POISSONS

BOURRIDE

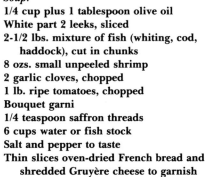

Rouille:
2 slices bread, soaked in milk
3 garlic cloves
1 teaspoon paprika
1/4 teaspoon cayenne pepper
1/4 cup plus 1 tablespoon olive oil
1 tablespoon plus 1 teaspoon tomato paste

Soup:
1/4 cup plus 1 tablespoon olive oil
White part 2 leeks, sliced
2-1/2 lbs. mixture of fish (whiting, cod, haddock), cut in chunks
8 ozs. small unpeeled shrimp
2 garlic cloves, chopped
1 lb. ripe tomatoes, chopped
Bouquet garni
1/4 teaspoon saffron threads
6 cups water or fish stock
Salt and pepper to taste
Thin slices oven-dried French bread and shredded Gruyère cheese to garnish

To prepare rouille, squeeze milk from bread. In a mortar, pound soaked bread and garlic to a paste. Add paprika and cayenne, then add oil drop by drop until blended. Beat in tomato paste. To prepare soup, heat oil in a very large saucepan. Cook leeks in oil until soft. Stir in shrimp and fish, turning in oil to coat. Cook over high heat until beginning to brown. Stir in garlic and tomatoes. Cover and cook gently 10 minutes. Add bouquet garni, saffron and water. Bring to a boil and simmer 30 minutes.

Remove bouquet garni. Strain soup. In a blender, process solids and a small amount of stock to a puree. Pour mixture through a sieve set over a bowl. Add 1/4 cup of fish soup to rouille and mix until smooth. Clean pan and reheat soup. Season with salt and pepper. Spread rouille on bread and top with cheese. Garnish soup with bread. Makes 6 servings.

Aioli:
4 garlic cloves
2 egg yolks
Pinch salt
1-1/4 cups olive oil

Soup:
2 lbs. firm white fish
2 leeks, sliced
2 garlic cloves
2 tomatoes, chopped
Orange peel strip
Bouquet garni
2/3 cup dry white wine
3-3/4 cups water or fish stock
Salt and peppper to taste
4 egg yolks
1/2 thin French bread, thinly sliced, dried in oven

To prepare aioli, pound garlic to a pulp in a mortar or crush with a garlic press and mash to a pulp with a wooden spoon. Place garlic in a small bowl and beat in egg yolks and salt. Add oil drop by drop, beating constantly. When 1/3 of oil has been used, add remainder more quickly until a thick mayonnaise is made. To prepare soup, clean fish and cut in large pieces. Place leeks, garlic, tomatoes, orange peel and bouquet garni in a large saucepan. Lay fish on top. Add wine and water and season with salt and pepper. Bring to a boil, then gently cook 10 to 15 minutes. Carefully remove fish and keep warm.

Strain stock through a sieve set over a bowl. In a large bowl, beat egg yolks into 1/2 of aioli. Add hot stock, whisking constantly. Clean pan and return soup to clean pan. Stir over low heat until soup thickens slightly. Do not allow soup to boil. To serve, arrange some bread slices in each soup bowl. Add fish and pour in soup. Spread extra slices of bread with remaining aioli and serve separately. Makes 6 servings.

VIETNAMESE SHRIMP SOUP

8 ozs. unpeeled cooked shrimp
1 bulb lemon grass, split in half lengthwise
1 (2-inch) piece gingerroot, peeled
3-3/4 cups light chicken stock
1 tablespoon lime juice
1/2 teaspoon crushed dried red chilies
1 tablespoon nam pla (fish sauce) or soy sauce
4 ozs. bok choy leaves, finely shredded

Peel shrimp and set aside. In a large saucepan, combine shells, lemon grass, gingerroot and stock. Bring to a boil. Simmer 5 minutes, then let stand 15 minutes.

Strain stock through a sieve set over a bowl. Clean pan and return stock to pan. Stir in lime juice, red chilies, nam pla and bok choy. Simmer 2 minutes.

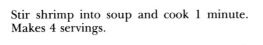

Stir shrimp into soup and cook 1 minute. Makes 4 servings.

COCK-A-LEEKIE

2 large chicken quarters
5 cups chicken stock
Bouquet garni
1 lb. leeks
12 prunes, soaked in water 1 hour
Salt and pepper to taste
Leek stems to garnish

Oaty Dumplings:
3/4 cup regular oats
1 cup whole-wheat bread crumbs
1 tablespoon chopped fresh herbs
Salt and pepper to taste
1/4 cup margarine, softened
2 to 3 tablespoons cold water

In a large saucepan, drop chicken into stock and add bouquet garni.

Bring to a boil, then simmer 30 minutes. Remove chicken from stock and cool. Remove bouquet garni and skim off any fat from surface of soup. Trim coarse leaves from leeks, then cut lengthwise. Wash thoroughly and cut in 1-inch pieces. Add leeks and prunes to soup. Simmer 25 minutes. Cut chicken in small pieces and add to soup. Season with salt and pepper.

To prepare dumplings, combine oats and bread crumbs in a medium-size bowl. Stir in herbs. Season with salt and pepper. Cut in margarine. Add cold water and mix to a dough. Divide in small balls and drop into soup. Cover and simmer 15 minutes. Garnish with leek stems. Makes 6 servings.

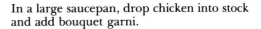

THAI CUCUMBER & PORK SOUP

4 dried Chinese mushrooms, soaked 20 minutes in hot water
3-3/4 cups chicken stock
6 ozs. pork tenderloin, cut in thin strips
1 tablespoon cornstarch
2 tablespoons soy sauce
2 tablespoons rice vinegar
1/2 cucumber, cut in thin strips
1-3/4 cups shredded Chinese cabbage

Remove stalks from mushrooms. Cut in thin slices. In a large saucepan, combine mushrooms and stock. Bring to a boil.

Place pork strips on a large plate. Sprinkle with cornstarch and roll lightly to coat. Add coated pork strips, soy sauce and vinegar to stock. Simmer 5 minutes.

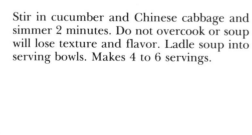

Stir in cucumber and Chinese cabbage and simmer 2 minutes. Do not overcook or soup will lose texture and flavor. Ladle soup into serving bowls. Makes 4 to 6 servings.

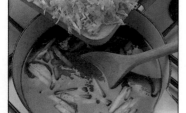

— CHICKEN NOODLE SOUP —

1 chicken carcass, raw or cooked, with giblets but not liver
1 small onion, sliced
1 large carrot, sliced
1 stalk celery, chopped
2 to 3 fresh parsley sprigs
1 teaspoon salt
6 black peppercorns
2 ozs. fine vermicelli
1 tablespoon finely chopped fresh parsley

To prepare stock, in a large deep saucepan, cover carcass with cold water and bring to a boil.

Skim off any scum that rises to surface. Add onion, carrot, celery and parsley sprigs and simmer gently 2-1/2 to 3 hours. Strain and cool carcass and stock. Refrigerate overnight. Remove any fat from surface of carcass. Measure 3-3/4 cups of stock into a large saucepan and reheat. Add salt and peppercorns.

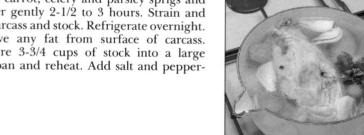

Crumble vermicelli into a pan of boiling salted water. Simmer 4 to 5 minutes. Drain and rinse. Place drained vermicelli in a soup tureen and cover with hot soup. Sprinkle with parsley. Makes 4 servings.

RICH COUNTRY CHICKEN SOUP

3 tablespoons butter
4 ozs. button mushrooms, chopped
1/3 cup all-purpose flour
2-1/2 cups strong chicken stock
2-1/2 cups milk
12 ozs. cooked chicken, diced
2 egg yolks
2/3 cup half and half
Salt and pepper to taste

Watercress Dumplings:
1 cup self-rising flour
1/2 teaspoon salt
Pinch mixed dried leaf herbs
2 ozs. shredded suet
1 bunch watercress, trimmed, finely chopped
1 small egg, beaten
1 tablespoon water
Chicken stock for cooking dumplings

Melt butter in a large saucepan. Gently cook mushrooms 4 to 5 minutes. Stir in flour, then gradually add stock and milk. Bring to a boil, stirring constantly. Cover and simmer 15 minutes. Meanwhile, to prepare dumplings, sift flour into a medium-size bowl. Mix in salt, herbs, suet and watercress. Add egg and water and mix to a dough. Roll dough in 24 balls. In a large saucepan, bring stock to a boil. Drop dumplings into stock, cover and simmer 10 minutes.

Remove soup from heat and stir in chicken. In a small bowl, beat egg yolks and half and half. Ladle in a small amount of soup into half and half mixture and mix quickly. Pour back into soup and heat gently without boiling until thick. Season with salt and pepper. Using a slotted spoon, remove dumplings from stock and add to soup to serve. Makes 6 servings.

PASSATELLI

5 cups well-flavored chicken stock
4 eggs
1 cup freshly grated Parmesan cheese (3 oz.)
1 cup fine dry white bread crumbs
1/4 teaspoon grated nutmeg
2 tablespoons butter, softened
Salt and pepper to taste

Bring stock to a boil in a large saucepan.

Beat eggs in a medium-size bowl. Stir in cheese, bread crumbs, nutmeg and butter. Season with salt and pepper. Mix to make a stiff paste.

Press paste through a colander into boiling stock. Cook 1 to 2 minutes or until threads of noodles rise to surface. Remove from heat and let stand 5 minutes before serving. Makes 4 servings.

SOUP GEORGETTE

2 tablespoons butter
1 medium-size onion, chopped
8 ozs. carrots, chopped
8 ozs. leeks, chopped
1 lb. tomatoes, peeled, coarsely chopped
3 cups chicken or vegetable stock
Small fresh rosemary sprig
Salt and pepper to taste
1/4 cup plus 2 tablespoons half and half
2 tomatoes and fresh rosemary sprigs
**   to garnish**

Melt butter in a large saucepan. Cook onion, carrots and leeks in butter 5 minutes. Stir in chopped tomatoes and cook 5 minutes.

Add stock and rosemary and bring to a boil. Cover and simmer 35 minutes. Remove rosemary. In a food processor fitted with a metal blade or a blender, process mixture to a puree. Clean pan and return puree to clean pan. Season with salt and pepper and stir in half and half.

Peel, seed and chop tomatoes. Garnish soup with chopped tomatoes and rosemary sprigs. Makes 4 servings.

ORIENTAL CHICKEN SOUP

Chicken Consommé:
4 ozs. minced veal
1 carrot, finely chopped
1 stalk celery, finely chopped
1 leek, trimmed, finely sliced
1 thyme sprig
1 bay leaf
7-1/2 cups chicken stock
Salt and pepper to taste
2 egg whites

Soup:
1 garlic clove, finely chopped
1 stalk lemon grass, cut in half lengthwise
Carrot flowers
2 green onions, sliced
2 ozs. cooked chicken breast, shredded
2 ozs. Chinese snow peas, trimmed, cut in
**   strips**

To prepare consommé, combine veal, vegetables, herbs and stock in a large saucepan. Season with salt and pepper and begin to heat. Whisk egg whites in a small bowl and pour into stock mixture, whisking continually until a thick froth begins to form. When stock mixture reaches boiling point, stop whisking and lower heat to maintain a very slow simmer. Do not allow mixture to boil. Cook consommé 1 hour.

Line a large sieve or colander with muslin and set over a bowl. Draw scum back from surface of consommé sufficiently to ladle liquid. Ladle clarified stock into muslin-lined sieve. Place a paper towel over surface to absorb any fat. Measure 3-3/4 cups consommé into a large saucepan. Add garlic and lemon grass and simmer 15 minutes. Meanwhile, blanch carrot flowers in boiling salted water 2 minutes. Remove lemon grass and add green onions, chicken and snow peas and simmer 2 minutes. Add carrot flowers just before serving. Makes 4 servings.

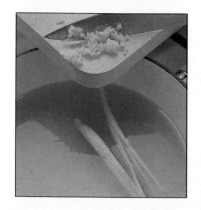

CHICKEN EGG DROP SOUP

1 tablespoon plus 2 teaspoons cornstarch
3 tablespoons rice wine
1 tablespoon soy sauce
5 cups chicken stock
1/2 teaspoon sugar
8 ozs. cooked chicken breast, diced
6 green onions, shredded
2 eggs
1 tablespoon plus 1 teaspoon all-purpose flour
Green onion curls to garnish

In a large saucepan, combine cornstarch, wine and soy sauce. Pour in stock and slowly bring to a boil. Simmer 2 minutes.

Add chicken and shredded green onions and simmer 2 to 3 minutes.

In a small bowl, beat eggs and flour. While stock is simmering, pour egg mixture through a sieve into stock. Simmer 1 minute, stirring stock as egg drops into pan. Garnish with green onion curls. Makes 4 to 6 servings.

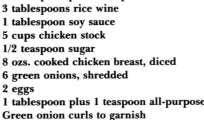

DEVILED TURKEY SOUP

1 tablespoon vegetable oil
1 medium-size onion, chopped
2 teaspoons curry powder
1/2 teaspoon dry mustard powder
12 oz. potatoes, diced
3-3/4 cups chicken stock
2 teaspoons Worcestershire sauce
6 oz. cooked turkey, diced
Salt and pepper to taste

Lemon Dumplings:
1 cup self-rising whole-wheat flour
Pinch salt
1/4 cup sunflower margarine
Grated peel and juice 1/2 lemon

Heat oil in a large saucepan. Gently cook onion in oil until soft. Stir in curry and dry mustard and cook 1 minute. Stir in potatoes and stock. Bring to a boil and simmer 30 minutes. Add Worcestershire sauce and turkey. Season with salt and pepper and slowly bring back to a simmer.

To prepare dumplings, place flour and salt in a medium-size bowl. Cut in margarine. Add lemon peel and juice and mix to a soft dough. Roll in small balls and drop into soup. Cover and cook 5 minutes or until balls are about double in size. Ladle into bowls and serve at once. Makes 4 servings.

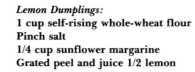

FENNEL & WALNUT SOUP

Sage Derby Puffs:
3 tablespoons water
2 tablespoons butter
1/4 cup all-purpose flour
1/2 egg, beaten
3/4 cup shredded Sage Derby cheese (3 oz.)
Salt and pepper to taste
1/2 (4-oz.) pkg. cream cheese
2 tablespoons half and half

Soup:
1 tablespoon vegetable oil
1 medium-size onion, chopped
1 large bulb fennel, trimmed, chopped
3-3/4 cups vegetable stock
2 oz. walnuts, chopped
Salt and pepper to taste

To prepare puffs, preheat oven to 400F (200C). Grease a baking sheet. In a medium-size saucepan, bring water and butter to a boil. Remove from heat and beat in flour until smooth. Cool slightly, then beat in egg. Stir in 1/2 of cheese. Season with salt and pepper. In a pastry bag fitted with a small plain nozzle, pipe pea-size rounds onto greased baking sheet. Bake in preheated oven 7 to 10 minutes or until crisp. Cool slightly, then cut a slit in each round with point of a sharp knife. To prepare soup, heat oil in a large saucepan. Gently cook onion and fennel in oil until soft. Add stock and bring to a boil, then simmer 20 minutes.

Meanwhile, beat remaining cheese, cream cheese and half and half in a small bowl. Fill slits in puffs. In a food processor fitted with a metal blade or a blender, grind walnuts. Transfer ground nuts to a small dish. In food processor or blender, process soup to a smooth puree. Clean pan and return puree to pan. Stir in ground nuts and season with salt and pepper. Gently reheat. Garnish with puffs. Makes 4 to 6 servings.

CONSOMMÉ MADRILENE

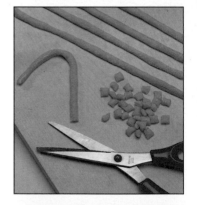

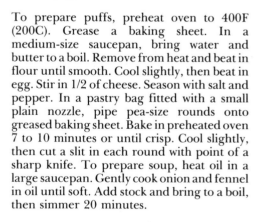

5 cups chicken stock
1 lb. tomatoes, chopped
4 stalks celery, finely chopped
1 (2-oz.) can chopped pimientos
1 lemon peel strip
2 egg whites
2 tablespoons dry sherry
2 ozs. pimientos, diced
1 tomato, peeled, diced
Salt and pepper to taste

Soup Nuts:
2 teaspoons vegetable oil
1/2 teaspoon salt
1 egg
3/4 cup all-purpose flour
Additional oil for frying

To prepare consommé, combine stock, tomatoes, celery, pimientos and lemon peel in a large saucepan. Whisk in egg whites. Bring to a boil, stirring constantly, then simmer very slowly 1 hour. To prepare Soup Nuts, place 2 tablespoons oil, salt and egg into a food processor fitted with a metal blade. Add flour and process to a smooth dough. Roll out dough in thin rolls about 1/4 inch thick and let dry 10 minutes. With scissors, snip rolls in 1/4-inch pieces and let dry 30 minutes.

Heat oil in a deep medium-size skillet. Fry dough pieces until crisp and golden. Drain on paper towels. Strain consommé through a muslin-lined sieve set over a bowl. Clean pan and return strained consommé to clean pan. Stir in sherry, pimientos and tomato. Season with salt and pepper and reheat. Serve soup with Soup Nuts. Makes 4 to 6 servings.

NEW ENGLAND CLAM CHOWDER

TOMATO & RICE SOUP

2 (10-oz.) cans clams
3 slices bacon, diced
1 medium-size onion, finely chopped
1 lb. potatoes, diced
1-1/4 cups fish stock
1-1/4 cups milk
2/3 cup half and half
Pinch dried leaf thyme
Salt and pepper to taste

Drain clams, reserving liquid. Chop clams and set aside.

Fry bacon in a large saucepan over high heat until fat runs and bacon in lightly browned. Add onion and saute until soft. Stir in reserved clam liquid, potatoes, stock and milk. Bring to a boil and simmer about 20 minutes or until potatoes are tender.

Stir in clams, half and half, and thyme. Season with salt and pepper. Reheat a few minutes, but do not allow to boil. Makes 6 servings.

1 small onion, chopped
2 garlic cloves, crushed
1 (1-lb./12-oz.) can tomatoes
2 tablespoons tomato paste
1 tablespoon chopped fresh basil or 1/2
   teaspoon dried leaf basil
2-1/2 cups water
1 teaspoon sugar
1/3 cup long-grain white rice
3 tablespoons dry sherry
Salt and pepper to taste
Fresh basil leaves to garnish

In a large saucepan, combine onion, garlic, tomatoes with juice, tomato paste, chopped basil, water and sugar. Bring to a boil, cover and simmer 30 minutes. In a food processor fitted with a metal blade or a blender, process tomato mixture to a puree. Clean pan. Pour puree through a sieve set over clean pan.

Bring back to a boil and add rice. Reduce heat and simmer 15 minutes or until rice is tender. Stir in sherry and season with salt and pepper. Garnish with basil leaves. Makes 4 to 6 servings.

PISTOU

1 tablespoon olive oil
1 medium-size onion, chopped
5 cups water
1 small potato, diced
2 carrots, sliced
2 stalks celery, finely sliced
Bouquet garni
2 small zucchini, sliced
6 ozs. green beans, cut in short lengths
1 oz. broken spaghetti or pasta shells
Salt and pepper to taste

Pistou:
3 garlic cloves
1/4 cup chopped fresh basil leaves
Salt to taste
1/2 cup freshly grated Parmesan cheese
　　(1-1/2 ozs.)
2 medium-size tomatoes, peeled, seeded,
　　chopped
1/4 cup olive oil

Heat 1 tablespoon oil in a large saucepan.
Cook onion in oil until onion is just beginning
to color. Pour in water and bring to a boil.
Add potato, carrots, celery and bouquet
garni. Simmer 10 minutes. Add zucchini,
green beans and pasta and simmer uncovered
10 to 15 minutes or until tender.

Meanwhile, to prepare pistou, pound garlic
and basil in a mortar with a pestle. Season
with salt. Gradually add cheese until mixture
becomes a stiff paste, then add about 1/3 of
tomatoes. Continue adding cheese and tomatoes alternately, then slowly work in remaining oil to make a thick sauce. Remove bouquet
garni from soup. Season with salt and pepper.
Serve soup with pistou. Makes 4 to 6 servings.

PESTO SOUP

1/4 cup plus 3 tablespoons olive oil
1 small onion, finely chopped
12 ounces zucchini, diced
1/2 cup rissotto rice
5 cups hot chicken stock
Salt and pepper to taste
1 oz. fresh basil leaves
1/4 cup pine nuts
2 garlic cloves
1/4 teaspoon salt
1/2 cup freshly grated Parmesan cheese

Parmesan Croutons:
2 tablespoons butter
2 slices bread

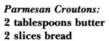

Heat 2 tablespoons of oil in a large saucepan.
Gently cook onion and zucchini 3 to 4 minutes or until softened. Stir in rice and coat
grains with oil. Pour in hot stock and bring to
a boil. Simmer 10 minutes or until rice is
tender. Season with salt and pepper. Meanwhile, to prepare pesto sauce, process
remaining olive oil, basil leaves, pine nuts,
garlic and 1/4 teaspoon salt to a puree in a
blender. Transfer mixture to a small bowl and
beat in 1/2 of cheese.

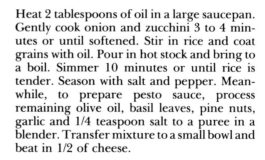

To prepare croutons, beat remaining cheese
and butter in a small bowl. Toast bread on
both sides. Spread toast with cheese-butter
and broil until melted and golden. Cut out
fancy shapes or remove crusts and dice. Stir 1
heaping tablespoon of pesto sauce into soup.
Refrigerate remaining pesto sauce for another use. Garnish soup with croutons. Makes
4 to 5 servings.

SUMMER TOMATO BISQUE

2 lbs. ripe tomatoes, chopped
3 green onions, chopped
1/2 red bell pepper, seeded, chopped
2 garlic cloves, crushed
2 cups vegetable stock
1 teaspoon sugar
2 tablespoons chopped fresh basil
1/4 cup crème fraiche or plain yogurt
Salt and pepper to taste
1 avocado and snipped chives to garnish

In a large saucepan, combine tomatoes, green onions, bell pepper, garlic, stock and sugar. Bring to a boil, then simmer 15 minutes. Remove from heat and cool.

In a food processor fitted with a metal blade or a blender, process mixture to a puree. Press puree through a sieve set over a bowl. Cover and refrigerate 2 hours to chill. Stir in basil and crème fraiche. Season with salt and pepper.

Cut avocado in half. Remove seed, peel and slice. Ladle soup into individual bowls. Arrange avocado slices on soup and sprinkle with snipped chives. Makes 6 servings.

SUMMER AVOCADO SOUP

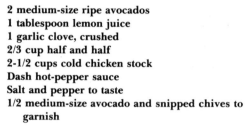

2 medium-size ripe avocados
1 tablespoon lemon juice
1 garlic clove, crushed
2/3 cup half and half
2-1/2 cups cold chicken stock
Dash hot-pepper sauce
Salt and pepper to taste
1/2 medium-size avocado and snipped chives to garnish

Cut 2 avocados in half. Remove seeds and scoop flesh into a food processor fitted with a metal blade or a blender. Add lemon juice, garlic and half and half and process to a puree.

Blend in stock and hot-pepper sauce. Season with salt and pepper.

Pour into a bowl. Cover to prevent discoloration and refrigerate 1 hour. Dice avocado half. Garnish soup with diced avocado and snipped chives. Makes 4 to 6 servings.

PUMPKIN SOUP

1 (3-lb.) pumpkin
2 tablespoons butter
1 medium-size onion, chopped
2-1/2 cups chicken stock
1 teaspoon light-brown sugar
2/3 cup half and half
1/4 teaspoon paprika
Good pinch grated nutmeg
Salt and pepper to taste

Paprika Niblets:
3 slices bread
Oil for frying
Paprika

Discard pumpkin seeds and stringy bits.

Cut out pumpkin flesh and dice. Melt butter in a large saucepan. Cook onion in butter until soft. Add diced pumpkin, stock and brown sugar. Bring to a boil, then simmer 30 minutes. In a food processor fitted with a metal blade or a blender, process mixture to a puree. Clean pan and return puree to clean pan. Stir in half and half, paprika and nutmeg. Season with salt and pepper. Reheat slowly.

Meanwhile, cut out attractive shapes from bread or make rings using 2 cutters, 1 slightly larger than other. Heat 1/4-inch of oil in a medium-size skillet and fry bread until golden. Drain on paper towels, then dust with paprika. Garnish soup with fried bread. Makes 6 servings.

COOL CHERRY SOUP

1-1/2 lbs. ripe black or red cherries
2/3 cup fruity white wine
1 (4-inch) piece cinnamon stick
2/3 cup water
2 tablespoons sugar
Grated peel and juice 1 lemon
1-1/4 cups dairy sour cream
2 tablespoons brandy, if desired

Remove stems and pits from cherries. Crush 1/2 of pits with a mallet.

In a large saucepan, combine crushed pits, whole pits, stems, wine, cinnamon, water, sugar and lemon peel and juice. Bring to a boil, cover and simmer 10 minutes. Strain liquid. Return to pan. Reserve 1/4 of cherries. Stir remaining cherries into strained liquid and simmer 5 minutes.

In a food processor fitted with a metal blade or a blender, process cherry mixture to a puree. Refrigerate until cool, then whisk in sour cream and brandy, if desired. Chill until ready to serve. Garnish soup with reserved cherries. Makes 4 to 6 servings.

ICED MELON SOUP

CHILLED PLUM SOUP

1 (1-1/2-lb.) honeydew melon
1 (1-1/2 lb.) cantaloupe
2-1/2 cups water
1 small piece gingerroot, peeled
1/2 cup sugar
1 cup dry white wine

Cut melons in half and discard seeds. Scoop out a few small balls from honeydew melon and set aside. Scoop remaining flesh from melons, keeping 2 varieties separate.

1 lb. red plums
2 cups water
2/3 cup fruity white wine
1/3 cup light-brown sugar
1 tablespoon lemon juice
Pinch ground cloves
2/3 cup buttermilk
1/2 teaspoon grated lemon peel
Lemon peel twists to garnish

In a large saucepan, combine plums, water, wine, brown sugar, lemon juice and cloves. Simmer gently about 10 minutes or until plums are tender.

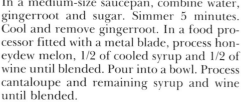

In a medium-size saucepan, combine water, gingerroot and sugar. Simmer 5 minutes. Cool and remove gingerroot. In a food processor fitted with a metal blade, process honeydew melon, 1/2 of cooled syrup and 1/2 of wine until blended. Pour into a bowl. Process cantaloupe and remaining syrup and wine until blended.

Press mixture through a sieve set over a bowl. Discard skin and pits from plums.

Chill both bowls of soup at least 1 hour. To serve, pour honeydew melon soup into individual bowls. Pour cantaloupe soup into middle of honeydew melon soup. Garnish with reserved melon balls. Makes 4 to 6 servings.

Refrigerate until chilled. Stir in buttermilk and grated lemon peel. Freeze soup 1 hour before serving and serve icy cold. Garnish soup with lemon peel twists. Makes 4 to 6 servings.

SANDWICHES

Introduction

The sandwich is said to have been invented by the fourth Earl of Sandwich, an inveterate gambler, who, when hungry at his card table demanded 'Bring me my beef between two slices of bread'. The idea caught on and sandwiches are still popular with those who, like the Earl, want to catch a quick bite.

In this section there are a wide variety of sandwiches suitable for many occasions, including quick hot snacks, afternoon teas or hors d'oeuvres. Small sandwiches make an excellent choice for light buffet lunches and cocktail parties and can be cut overnight and left in the fridge with the filling. You can be extravagant if your budget will allow, but even thrifty canapés look pretty and taste epicurean. Egg-Chive Tea Sandwiches, Celery Pâté Sticks and Mini Rye Clubs are inexpensive to prepare but make an impressive show. A Party Sandwich Cake is an eye-catching centerpiece to any table.

For a more substantial sandwich-based lunch party, create a Scandinavian style *smorgasbord*. This consists of a selection of open-faced sandwiches usually on a variety of different breads such as pumpernickel, rye and crispbreads. Potted Shrimp Treat, Salami Sandwich, Gravlax Slice and Stilton-Pear Topper would be good choices. Again, this is an informal meal but looks appetizing and plentiful. It would make a perfect arrangement for a special birthday party or anniversary celebration.

Bread types have been suggested in this section for various recipes, however use the breads that you enjoy most. As a guideline, it is best to make substantial sandwiches with thick slices of crunchy bread, delicate canapés with thin slices of crustless light bread, while open sandwiches need a firm textured bread like rye or pumpernickel. There is an amazing variety of breads on sale. In addition to the more familiar white loaf, either seeded or plain, and the higher fiber wholewheat loaves, there is also brown bread containing some wheat bran and possibly additional caramel coloring, which, fiber-wise, has little advantage over white bread. Granary loaves are popular and these are baked from special malted flours with additional whole or cracked grains.

Small bakeries often sell their own special bread, while some health food stores have a bakery attached and sell a selection of wholesome breads based on unusual mixtures of flours and grains. Continental and ethnic food stores also sell fabulous breads whose origins are in central Europe and Italy – even the familiar French stick is available in traditional white, granary and wholewheat varieties. Look out for rich Jewish Egg Bread, German style Pumpernickel with its heavy coarse texture, Arabian bread and Irish soda bread.

Bread freezes well, although with very crusty bread, there is a likelihood that the crust will separate from the loaf after freezing. Always freeze and defrost bread as quickly as possible to prevent staling and minimise crust separation. Supermarkets sell part-baked bread, either vacuum sealed or frozen, which are excellent to have in reserve and when cooked, have a delicious freshness about them. Eat as soon as possible after baking as this type of bread has poor keeping qualities.

Butter is placed between bread partly for taste, and partly as a barrier to prevent moisture from the filling making the bread damp. Low fat spreads and margarines serve the same function and may be substituted for butter, when making the sandwiches illustrated in the book. For a delicious change, try flavoring butter. However, keep in mind that the flavored butter should complement the filling. For example, try horseradish butter with beef. Simply beat the flavoring into softened butter or margarine and spread over bread slices before adding fillings.

There are several measures that can be taken to keep sandwiches cool and edible on the hottest of days. Prepare the fillings in advance and cut the bread. Wrap the bread in plastic wrap and foil to freeze. Make the sandwich with the frozen bread, and you will find that it will have thawed by lunchtime and will have also kept the filling cool. Alternatively, pack the sandwich next to a frozen can of fruit juice wrapped in a plastic bag.

Children will think that Ham & Pineapple Muffins and Chicken Maryland Rolls are great fun, and nutritionally they both contain plenty of protein and a variety of vitamins and fiber, especially if prepared with wholewheat rolls and muffins. Even the recipe for Peanut-Banana Malties is a healthy choice.

Some of the canapé-style sandwiches are very attractive to children, for example, Cheese-Cress Pinwheels, Traffic Lights and French Toast Fingers. If you are having a children's party, cut the sandwiches into shapes with a dough cutter. It is easy to make the sandwiches into a selection of letters, geometric shapes or animals. To accompany the sandwiches, try and make biscuits following the same theme. Shaped sandwiches may also make lunch boxes more exciting if you have a reluctant eater on your hands.

— Indian Spiced Chicken on Nan Bread —

1 small eggplant, trimmed, diced
1-1/2 teaspoons salt
1/4 cup corn oil
1 lb. skinned boneless chicken breasts,
    cut in thin strips
1 green bell pepper, seeded, diced
2 medium-size onions, cut in half, then
    thinly sliced
1 (2-inch) piece gingerroot, peeled, finely
    chopped
1 teaspoon ground cumin
1 teaspoon ground coriander
1/4 teaspoon turmeric
1/2 teaspoon chili powder
1/2 teaspoon ground cinnamon
2 garlic cloves, crushed
3 tablespoons plain yogurt
3 tablespoons cold water
2 nan breads
3 tablespoons butter, softened
2 tomatoes, peeled, seeded, cut in slivers
Sprigs of fresh cilantro to garnish

In a colander, layer eggplant with 1 teaspoon of salt. Drain over a plate 30 minutes. Rinse well and pat dry on paper towels. Heat 2 tablespoons of oil in a medium-size saucepan. Add chicken and stir-fry 3 minutes. Remove chicken from pan. Add remaining oil to pan. Heat oil and add eggplant, bell pepper, onions, gingerroot, spices and garlic. Stir-fry 3 minutes. Add chicken and stir in remaining salt, yogurt and cold water. Cover and cook 10 minutes, stirring occasionally. Meanwhile, toast breads until lightly golden and heated through. Butter bread. Cut each buttered bread in 2 or 3 serving pieces. Stir tomatoes into chicken mixture. Serve hot on buttered bread. Garnish with cilantro. Makes 4 to 6 pieces.

— Vegetable Curry Pies —

2 tablespoons corn oil
1 medium-size baking potato, grated
1 medium-size onion, chopped
1 medium-size carrot, grated
1 stalk celery, chopped
1 teaspoon cumin seeds
1 garlic clove, crushed
1-1/2 to 2 teaspoons curry powder
1 teaspoon fresh lemon juice
2 tablespoons frozen green peas
3 tablespoons frozen corn
1/4 cup chicken stock
Salt to taste
8 medium-thick slices white bread,
    crusts removed
1/3 cup butter, softened
1 tablespoon poppy seeds
Sprigs of fresh cilantro to garnish

Heat oil in a medium-size saucepan. Fry potato, onion, carrot and celery 3 minutes. Add cumin, garlic and curry powder; fry 2 minutes. Stir in lemon juice, peas, corn and chicken stock. Season with salt. Mix well. Cover and simmer 10 minutes. Meanwhile, preheat oven to 375F (190C). Using a rolling pin, firmly flatten slices of bread. Butter 4 slices on 1 side and remaining 4 on both sides. Press slices of bread buttered on both sides into 4 (4-inch) round pans. Trim edges. Fill with vegetable mixture. Using a 1-1/2-inch round fluted cutter, cut 9 rounds from each slice of bread buttered on 1 side. Place bread rounds, buttered sides up, in an overlapping border around edge of vegetable mixture. Press down lightly. Sprinkle poppy seeds around each bread round. Bake in preheated oven 15 to 20 minutes or until bread is golden brown. Garnish with cilantro. Serve hot. Makes 4 pies.

Pita Lamb Keftadas

1 slice whole-wheat bread, crusts
  removed
1 tablespoon cold water
8 ozs. lean lamb, minced
1 small onion, finely chopped
2 tablespoons beaten egg
2 teaspoons fresh lemon juice
1/2 teaspoon dried leaf thyme
1/2 teaspoon dried leaf oregano
2 tablespoons chopped fresh mint
Salt and pepper to taste
Vegetable oil for frying
1/4 cucumber, sliced lengthwise, cut
  in strips
3 green onions, chopped
1/4 red bell pepper, seeded, chopped
2/3 cup plain yogurt
2 large pita breads
Lemon wedges and sprigs of fresh mint
  to garnish

In a medium-size bowl, soak bread in cold water 5 minutes, then crumble bread. Add lamb, onion, egg, 1 teaspoon of lemon juice, thyme, oregano and 1 tablespoon of chopped mint. Season with salt and pepper. Mix well. Using well-floured hands, form mixture in small balls the size of a walnut. Heat oil in a large skillet. Fry meatballs 10 to 12 minutes or until golden. Drain on paper towels. In a small bowl, combine cucumber, green onions and bell pepper. In another small bowl, mix yogurt with remaining lemon juice and mint. Season with salt and pepper. Mix well. Stir 2 tablespoons of yogurt mixture into cucumber mixture. Toast pita bread until warmed through. Cut a slice off long edge of each and open to form pockets. Spoon cucumber salad into pockets and fill with meatballs. Top with a small amount of yogurt mixture. Garnish with lemon wedges and sprigs of mint and serve hot with remaining yogurt sauce. Makes 2 sandwiches.

Chicken Chili Tacos

3 tablespoons corn oil
1 medium-size onion, chopped
1 garlic clove, crushed
1-1/2 teaspoons chili powder
1/2 teaspoon ground cumin
3/4 lb. skinned boneless chicken breast,
  finely chopped or minced
2 tablespoons tomato paste
1/2 (4-oz.) can chopped green chilies,
  drained
2/3 cup chicken stock
2 teaspoons cornstarch
1 tablespoon cold water
6 taco shells
Finely shredded lettuce leaves
Slivered onion
Chopped tomatoes
Sour cream

Preheat oven to 350F (175C). Heat oil in a medium-size skillet. Add onion, garlic, chili powder, cumin and chicken. Saute 4 to 5 minutes, stirring frequently. Stir in tomato paste, green chilies and chicken stock. Simmer 10 minutes, stirring occasionally. In a 1-cup glass measure, combine cornstarch and cold water. Stir into chicken mixture. Cook 2 minutes, stirring constantly. Meanwhile, heat taco shells in preheated oven following package directions. Fill hot taco shells with chicken mixture. Top with shredded lettuce, slivered onion and tomatoes. Add a dollop of sour cream. Serve at once. Makes 6 tacos.

Variation: Substitute lean ground beef or minced pork for chicken.

Steak Sandwich

3 tablespoons butter
1 thick slice crusty whole-wheat or
    white bread
1 medium-size onion, cut in half, then
    thinly sliced
1 garlic clove, crushed
1/4 lb. sirloin steak, cut in thin strips
2 tablespoons whipping cream
1 tablespoon water
1 teaspoon tomato paste
1 to 2 teaspoons chopped fresh chives
1/4 teaspoon prepared mustard
Salt and pepper to taste
Small onion rings and chives to garnish

Butter bread with 1 tablespoon of butter. Heat remaining butter in a medium-size skillet. Add onion; saute 2 minutes. Increase heat to medium high. Add garlic and steak. Fry until steak is cooked as desired, stirring frequently. Using a slotted spoon, remove steak and onion to a plate and keep warm. To prepare sauce, stir whipping cream, water, tomato paste, chopped chives and mustard into juices in skillet. Bring to a boil, stirring to scrape sediment in skillet. Season with salt and pepper. Simmer 30 seconds. Spoon steak and onions onto buttered bread and drizzle with sauce. Garnish with onion rings and chives. Serve at once. Makes 1 sandwich.

Greek Salad Pitas

1/2 cup plus 2 tablespoons olive oil
2 tablespoons fresh lemon juice
1 garlic clove, crushed
1/4 teaspoon sugar
1 teaspoon chopped fresh oregano
Salt and pepper to taste
1/4 head Romaine lettuce, shredded
1 small red onion, sliced, then separated
    in rings
1/4 cucumber, thinly sliced
1 large tomato, cut in quarters, then
    sliced
1/2 small green bell pepper, seeded, cut
    in slivers
4 ozs. feta cheese, cut in cubes or fingers
4 large pita breads
12 pitted black olives
Lemon twists and sprigs of fresh Italian
    parsley to garnish

To make dressing, in a large bowl, whisk olive oil, lemon juice, garlic, sugar and oregano. Season with salt and pepper. Add shredded lettuce, onion, cucumber, tomato, bell pepper and cheese. Toss lightly until coated with dressing. Lightly toast pita breads. Cut a slice off long edge of each and open to form pockets. Generously fill each pita with salad mixture, allowing mixture to rise above top edges of breads. Add olives to each. Garnish with lemon twists and parsley. Makes 4 sandwiches.

Variation: Add peeled cooked shrimp to salad and toss with dressing.

Chili Dogs

3 tablespoons corn oil
1 small onion, thinly sliced
1 garlic clove, crushed
1 teaspoon chili powder
1 (8-oz.) can tomatoes, drained, chopped
1 tablespoon tomato paste
1/2 teaspoon dry mustard
1 tablespoon malt vinegar
1 tablespoon Worcestershire sauce
1 tablespoon soft light-brown sugar
1/4 teaspoon salt
1 (8-oz.) can barbecue beans
4 frankfurters
4 seeded hotdog rolls
1/4 cup butter, softened
Onion rings
Snipped green onion stems and fresh
   cress to garnish

To prepare chili sauce, heat 2 tablespoons of oil in a medium-size saucepan. Add onion, garlic and chili powder; saute 2 minutes. Stir in tomatoes, tomato paste, dry mustard, malt vinegar, Worcestershire sauce, brown sugar and salt. Simmer 5 minutes. Stir in beans; cook 5 minutes. Meanwhile, preheat broiler. Cut frankfurters alternately on both sides at 1/2-inch intervals. Brush with remaining oil. Broil under preheated broiler 3 to 4 minutes or until browned, turning frequently. Cut rolls lengthwise, but do not cut through. Open and spread with butter. Place frankfurters in rolls. Arrange onion rings along 1 side of each frankfurter. Spoon chili sauce over frankfurters. Garnish with green onion stems and cress. Makes 4 chili dogs.

Giant Salad Burgers

1 lb. lean ground beef
3 tablespoons corn oil
Salt and pepper to taste
2 seeded rolls
2 green onions
3 tablespoons mayonnaise
2 tablespoons mango chutney
2 thick slices lettuce
2 slices large tomato
4 red bell pepper rings
Mild pickled chilies and tomatoes, to
   garnish

Form beef in 2 (4-inch) round patties. Heat oil in a medium-size skillet. Fry patties 5 to 6 minutes on each side or until cooked as desired. Season with salt and pepper. Cut rolls in half and lightly toast. Cut green onions in half. Using a sharp pointed knife, cut to form feathery ends. In a small bowl, mix mayonnaise and chutney. Spread bottom half of rolls with 1/2 of mayonnaise mixture. Arrange slices of lettuce on rolls. Top with slices of tomato. Place patties on tomato slices. Cover with green onions and bell pepper rings. Spoon remaining mayonnaise mixture over green onions and bell pepper rings. Cover with top half of rolls. To garnish, thread wooden picks with pickled chilies and tomatoes; push into each burger. Makes 2 burgers.

Variations: Omit mayonnaise mixture and top with ketchup or relish.

Add a slice of processed cheese or thin slices of Gruyère cheese.

Welsh Rarebit

2 tablespoons butter
1-1/4 cups grated Cheddar cheese
1 teaspoon milk
1/4 teaspoon dry mustard
Few drops Worcestershire sauce
1/8 teaspoon cayenne pepper
Salt to taste
2 crusty slices whole-wheat bread
Tomato wedges and sprigs of fresh
    watercress to garnish

Melt 1 tablespoon of butter in a small saucepan. Remove from heat. Add cheese, milk, dry mustard, Worcestershire sauce and cayenne pepper. Season with salt. Mix well. Cook over low heat for a few moments until mixture begins to melt, stirring constantly. Remove from heat. Preheat broiler. Toast

bread. Spread with remaining butter. Spread cheese mixture on buttered toast. Broil under preheated broiler 3 to 4 minutes or until golden and bubbling. Garnish with tomato wedges and watercress sprigs and serve hot. Makes 2 sandwiches.

Variation: To prepare *Bacon-Broccoli Rarebit*, cook 8 small fresh broccoli spears in a small amount of boiling salted water 5 minutes or until just tender. Drain well on paper towels. Cut off stalk so that broccoli spears fit on toast. Fry strips of bacon until crisp and golden. Place bacon over buttered toast. Top with broccoli spears and coat with cheese mixture. Broil until golden and bubbling.

Croque Monsieur

3 tablespoons butter, softened
2 (1/2-inch-thick) slices white bread,
    crusts removed
1 slice cooked ham
2 thin slices Gruyère cheese
Sprigs of fresh parsley to garnish

Lightly butter slices of bread on both sides. Cut ham and cheese slices to fit slices of bread. Place 1 slice of cheese and ham on 1 slice of buttered bread. Top with remaining slice of cheese and buttered bread. Press together firmly.

Cut diagonally in half. Heat a small skillet over low heat. Fry sandwich until cheese melts, pressing down occasionally during cooking. Turn once and cook until golden brown on both sides. Garnish with parsley. Serve hot. Makes 1 sandwich.

Variation: Substitute Cheddar cheese for Gruyère cheese. Spread cheese with pickle relish or ham with prepared mustard.

Scotch Egg Rolls

1/2 lb. pork sausage
1 small onion, finely chopped
Salt and pepper to taste
2 hard-cooked eggs, peeled
1 tablespoon all-purpose flour
1 egg, beaten
3 tablespoons dry bread crumbs
Vegetable oil for deep frying
4 round rolls
1/3 cup butter, softened
Chicory leaves
2 large tomatoes, thinly sliced
2 tablespoons piccalilli or hot dog relish
Crisp bacon rolls, radish flowers and
    additional chicory leaves to garnish

Place sausage and onion in a medium-size bowl. Season with salt and pepper. Mix well. Divide sausage mixture in half. Roll hard-cooked eggs in flour and flour hands. Wrap eggs in sausage mixture to enclose completely. Dip in beat-en egg and roll in bread crumbs. Press bread crumbs on firmly. Half-fill a deep saucepan with oil. Heat to 375F (190C) or until a 1-inch cube of day-old bread browns in 40 seconds. Fry eggs 6 minutes or until golden. Drain on paper towels and cool. Cut off tops of rolls. Butter tops. Cut a thin slice from bottoms of rolls; spread each cut side with butter. Scoop out centers of rolls large enough to place half an egg; discard centers. Spread center sections with butter. Cover buttered bottom slices with chicory leaves and tomato slices. Place center sections on bottoms. Cut eggs in half; press into centers of rolls. Spoon on piccalilli. Place buttered tops at an angle. To garnish, thread 4 wooden picks with bacon rolls, radish flowers and additional chicory leaves; push into each roll. Makes 4 rolls.

Egg & Bacon Rolls

6 slices bacon
2 long crusty rolls
3 tablespoons butter, softened
Tomato relish or chili sauce
Chicory or red leaf lettuce leaves
2 small tomatoes, sliced
2 hard-cooked eggs, sliced
Salt and pepper to taste
1 tablespoon mayonnaise, if desired
Sprigs of fresh parsley to garnish

In a medium-size skillet, fry bacon until crisp. Drain on paper towels. Meanwhile, partially slice rolls lengthwise; do not cut through bottom crust. Open and spread each cut side with butter. Spoon a small amount of tomato relish along sides of rolls. Arrange chicory leaves along 1 side of rolls and tomato slices along other side. Place egg slices in an overlapping row next to tomato slices. Season with salt and pepper. Spread egg slices with mayonnaise, if desired. Top with bacon. Garnish with parsley. Makes 2 rolls.

Variation: Substitute slices of cooked cold sausage for bacon.

Cheesy Garlic Bread

1 short loaf French bread
1/2 cup butter, softened
1 or 2 garlic cloves, crushed
1 tablespoon chopped fresh herbs
   (chives, parsley, chervil)
1 teaspoon fresh lemon juice
1/2 cup grated Red Leicester or Cheddar
   cheese
4 slices cooked ham, cut in quarters
Sprigs of fresh herbs to garnish

Preheat oven to 375F (190C). Cut bread in 4 equal pieces. Cut each piece in 4 thick slices; do not to cut through bottom crust. In a small bowl, mix butter, garlic, chopped herbs, lemon juice and 1/2 of cheese until well combined.

Spread cheese mixture between each slice of bread and at each cut end, reserving a small amount to spread on tops. Fold ham quarters and place between bread slices. Place pieces of bread on individual pieces of foil. Butter top of each with remaining butter mixture. Enclose each piece tightly in foil. Bake in preheated oven 15 minutes. Open foil and sprinkle with remaining cheese. Return to oven and bake 6 minutes or until cheese melts. Garnish with herbs and serve hot. Makes 4 pieces.

Variation: Substitute garlic sausage or salami for ham.

Stuffed French Bread

4 ozs. sliced garlic sausage, chopped
1/2 cup salted cashews, chopped
4 green onions, chopped
1 small green bell pepper, seeded,
   chopped
2 stalks celery, chopped
1 (8-oz.) package cream cheese with
   chives, softened
1 tablespoon plus 1 teaspoon tomato
   paste
1 garlic clove, crushed
Salt and pepper to taste
1 thin loaf French bread
Green onion flowers and small tomato
   roses to garnish

In a medium-size bowl, mix garlic sausage, cashews, chopped green onions, bell pepper, celery, cream cheese, tomato paste and garlic. Season with salt and pepper. Mix well. Cut bread in half crosswise, then cut off crusty ends. Using a sharp pointed knife, cut away soft bread from inside of each half, leaving shell intact. Using a teaspoon, fill centers of bread halves with cream cheese mixture, pushing in well from both ends to prevent any gaps in filling. Wrap each half individually in foil. Refrigerate 2 hours. Cut each half in 10 slices. Garnish with green onion flowers and tomato roses. Makes 20 pieces.

Saucy Seafood Loaf

1 short loaf French bread
1/3 cup butter
1 medium-size onion, finely chopped
1/2 cup all-purpose flour
1-1/4 cups milk
1/2 cup half and half
2 tablespoons dry white wine
6 ozs. peeled cooked fresh or frozen
   shrimp, thawed if frozen
6 ozs. cooked salmon steak
2 tablespoons chopped fresh parsley
Salt and pepper to taste
1/4 cup grated Emmentaler or Cheddar
   cheese
Lemon slices, unpeeled cooked shrimp
   and sprigs of fresh parsley to garnish

Preheat oven to 375F (190C). Cut bread lengthwise along top; do not cut through bottom. Open slightly. Remove soft bread from both sides, leaving shell intact. Prepare 3 tablespoons bread crumbs from soft bread. Melt 1/4 cup of butter in a medium-size saucepan. Add onion; saute 3 minutes. Stir in flour. Cook 1 minute, then gradually stir in milk and half and half. Bring to a boil, stirring constantly. Simmer 2 minutes. Add wine, peeled shrimp, salmon and chopped parsley. Season with salt and pepper. Mix well. Spoon seafood mixture into bread shell. Place a sheet of foil on a baking sheet. Place filled bread shell on foil. Melt remaining butter in a small saucepan. Remove from heat and mix in bread crumbs. Sprinkle buttered bread crumbs over seafood mixture in bread shell. Sprinkle with cheese. Wrap foil around sides of loaf, leaving top exposed. Bake in preheated oven 20 to 25 minutes or until topping is golden. Garnish with lemon slices, unpeeled shrimp and parsley sprigs. Cut in 4 pieces and serve hot. Makes 4 pieces.

New Orleans Oyster Loaf

12 fresh or bottled oysters
1/2 cup plus 2 tablespoons all-purpose
   flour
Salt and pepper to taste
1/8 teaspoon salt
3/8 teaspoon cayenne pepper
1 teaspoon corn oil
3 tablespoons cold water
1 egg white, beaten until stiff
Vegetable oil for deep frying
1 short loaf whole-wheat French bread
2/3 cup prepared tartar sauce
2 lettuce leaves, shredded
4 green onion flowers and lemon wedges
   to garnish

Pat oysters dry on paper towels. Dust with 2 tablespoons of flour. Season with salt and pepper. To make batter, in a medium-size bowl, mix remaining flour, 1/8 teaspoon salt, cayenne pepper, corn oil and cold water until thick. Fold beaten egg white into batter. Half-fill a deep saucepan with oil and heat to 375F (190C) or until 1 cube of day-old bread browns in 40 seconds. Dip prepared oysters into batter. Deep-fry oysters 3 to 4 minutes or until golden. Drain on paper towels and keep warm. Cut bread lengthwise 1/3 of way from top; do not cut completely through bottom. Remove most of soft bread. Spoon 2/3 of tartar sauce into bottom half of bread, spreading a small amount inside top half. Fill bottom half of bread with shredded lettuce. Season with salt and pepper. Place oysters on lettuce. Spoon remaining tartar sauce over oysters. Garnish with green onion flowers and lemon wedges. Cut in half and serve hot. Makes 2 sandwiches.

Chinese Salad Sticks

6 ozs. pork fillet, cut in thin strips
1 tablespoon sesame oil
2 garlic cloves, crushed
1 (1-inch) piece gingerroot, peeled, very
    finely chopped
2 tablespoons light soy sauce
Pepper to taste
2 tablespoons corn oil
4 green onions, cut diagonally in slices
1/2 red bell pepper, seeded, cut in thin
    slivers
12 small snow peas, ends and stems
    removed
1 French roll
1/4 cup butter, softened
Chicory leaves, torn in sprigs
2 ozs. fresh bean sprouts
Green onion flowers and additional
    slivers of red bell pepper to garnish

Put pork strips, 2 teaspoons of sesame oil, garlic, gingerroot and soy sauce into a medium-size bowl. Season with pepper. Mix well. Heat corn oil in a wok or medium-size skillet. Add pork mixture; stir-fry 4 to 5 minutes. Add green onions, bell pepper and snow peas; stir-fry 2 to 3 minutes. Remove from heat and keep warm. Cut roll in half lengthwise. If necessary, cut off a thin sliver of crust to make pieces of roll stand level. Spread with butter. Cover with chicory sprigs and bean sprouts. Top with hot pork mixture. Sprinkle with remaining sesame oil. Garnish with green onion flowers and additional bell pepper slivers. Serve at once. Makes 2 sandwiches.

Hummus Salad Bread Loaf

1/2 (15-1/2-oz.) can garbanzo beans,
    drained
2 garlic cloves
2 tablespoons olive oil
1 tablespoon tahini (creamed sesame)
2 tablespoons fresh lemon juice
1/8 teaspoon cayenne pepper
1/4 to 1/2 teaspoon ground cumin
1/2 teaspoon salt
2 tablespoons chopped fresh parsley
Pepper to taste
1 short loaf sesame seed French bread
1/4 cup butter, softened
1 red bell pepper, seeded, cut in rings
1/2 Spanish onion, sliced thinly, then
    separated in rings
1 oz. fresh bean sprouts
2 Chinese cabbage leaves, shredded
2 tablespoons French dressing
Sprigs of fresh parsley to garnish

In a food processor fitted with the metal blade or a blender, process garbanzo beans, garlic, olive oil, tahini, lemon juice, cayenne pepper, cumin, salt and chopped parsley until smooth. Season with pepper and additional salt, if desired. Cut bread in half lengthwise. Butter both bread halves, then spread bottom half of buttered bread with garbanzo bean mixture. Cover with bell pepper and onion rings. In a small bowl, toss bean sprouts and shredded cabbage in dressing. Drain and spoon over bell pepper and onion rings. Cover with top half of buttered bread. With fine string, tie in 4 places to hold loaf together. Cut in 4 thick pieces. Garnish with sprigs of parsley. Makes 4 pieces.

Pan Bagna

1/4 cup plus 2 tablespoons olive oil
2 tablespoons wine or malt vinegar
1 garlic clove, crushed
1/2 teaspoon Dijon-style mustard
1/2 teaspoon sugar
Salt and pepper to taste
1 short loaf French bread
1/4 head curly endive
4 medium-size tomatoes, sliced
8 green bell pepper rings
1 (6-oz.) can pimentos, drained, cut in
   thin strips
12 pitted black olives, cut in half
1 (2-oz.) can anchovy fillets, drained, cut
   in half lengthwise
1 tablespoon chopped fresh parsley
Sliced black olives and sprigs of fresh
   parsley to garnish

To make dressing, in a small bowl, whisk olive oil, wine vinegar, garlic, mustard and sugar. Season with salt and pepper. Mix until thoroughly combined. Cut bread in 4 pieces. Cut each piece in half lengthwise. Remove most of soft bread from each half. Brush with dressing. Arrange several endive leaves on bottom halves of bread. Dip tomatoes and bell pepper rings into remaining dressing and arrange over endive leaves. Arrange 1/2 of pimento strips over bell pepper rings. Top with halved olives and anchovy fillets. Sprinkle with chopped parsley. Cover with top halves of bread. Wrap each piece in foil. Place on a plate. Cover with another plate and weigh down with heavy weights. Refrigerate at least 1 hour before serving. Arrange remaining pimento strips in a crisscross pattern over tops of bread. Garnish with sliced olives and parsley. Makes 4 pieces.

Ham & Cheese Roll-Ups

1 thin loaf sesame seed French bread
1/4 cup butter, softened
1 teaspoon prepared mustard
2 to 3 tablespoons mayonnaise
3 square slices cooked ham
8 ozs. ricotta cheese
1 bunch cress, snipped
Salt and pepper to taste
18 thin slices cucumber
3 small tomatoes, thinly sliced
Sprigs of fresh watercress to garnish

Using a sharp knife, cut out 6 "V" shaped pieces at regular intervals along bread, deep and wide enough to hold a stuffed ham roll and cucumber and tomato slices. In a small bowl, mix butter and mustard. Spread butter mixture inside "V" shapes, then spread with mayonnaise. Spread ham slices with ricotta cheese. Arrange snipped cress, green parts facing outwards, along 2 opposite edges. Season with salt and pepper. Roll up ham to show green cress at ends. Cut each ham roll in half. Arrange overlapping cucumber and tomato slices in each "V" shaped cut. Place a ham roll in each "V" shape. Garnish with watercress. Cut in 6 thick slices. Makes 6 pieces.

Italian Meatball Hero

1 tablespoon olive oil
1 small onion, finely chopped
1 garlic clove, crushed
2 teaspoons dried leaf oregano
1 (8-oz.) can tomatoes, drained, chopped
1 tablespoon tomato paste
1 French roll
2/3 lb. lean ground beef
Salt and pepper to taste
Vegetable oil for frying
1/3 cup butter, softened
6 ozs. sliced mozzarella cheese
Sprigs of fresh watercress to garnish

To prepare tomato sauce, heat olive oil in a medium-size saucepan. Add onion, garlic, 1 teaspoon of oregano, tomatoes and tomato paste. Cook 10 minutes or until thick, stirring occasionally. Meanwhile, preheat oven to 375F (190C). Cut bread horizontally in half; do not cut through bottom crust. Remove all soft bread from center of both halves, leaving shell intact. Prepare 2 tablespoons of bread crumbs from soft bread. In a medium-size bowl, combine remaining bread crumbs and ground beef. Season with salt and pepper. Mix well. Form mixture in 12 small balls. Heat oil in a medium-size skillet. Add meatballs and fry 5 minutes or until set and golden. Drain on paper towels. Spread inside of bread shell with 2/3 of butter and add 1/2 of tomato sauce. Fill bread shell with meatballs and spoon sauce over meatballs. Cover with 1/2 of cheese slices. Press bread shell together. Spread outside of shell with remaining butter and cover with remaining slices of cheese and oregano. Wrap sandwich completely in greased foil. Bake in preheated oven 20 minutes. Unwrap foil to expose sandwich and bake 8 to 10 minutes more or until crisp. Cut in 4 thick pieces. Garnish with watercress. Makes 4 pieces.

Chilied Salami Hero

1/2 long French bread roll
3 tablespoons butter, softened
1 small garlic clove, crushed
1 to 2 tablespoons canned chopped green chilies
1/2 ripe avocado
1 teaspoon fresh lemon juice
4 slices salami, rinds removed
1 slice processed Cheddar cheese
Cherry tomatoes and pickled whole chilies to garnish

Cut roll lengthwise 2/3 way from bottom to top; do not cut through top crust. Open roll and remove center. In a small bowl, mix butter and garlic. Butter inside of roll. Sprinkle bottom of roll with chopped chilies. Peel avocado, cut in thin slices and dip into lemon juice. Arrange avocado slices along bottom of roll in a fan-shape. Fold salami slices in quarters. Arrange over avocado slices. Cut cheese slice diagonally in quarters and arrange along other side of roll. To garnish, thread 2 or 3 wooden picks with cherry tomatoes and pickled whole chilies; push into roll. Makes 1 sandwich.

── Peppered Salami-Slaw Sandwich ──

1/4 cup very finely shredded red cabbage
2 green onions, chopped
1 carrot, grated
1/3 cup fresh bean sprouts
2 tablespoons French dressing
1/4 cup butter, softened
4 thick slices whole-wheat or white bread
6 slices peppered salami
8 thin slices cucumber
1 large tomato, thinly sliced
Salt and pepper to taste
8 small tomato wedges and sprigs of
    fresh parsley to garnish

Rinse cabbage in cold water; drain well. In a medium-size bowl, combine cabbage, green onions, carrot, bean sprouts and dressing. Toss well. Butter bread. Arrange salami over 2 slices of buttered bread. Cover with cucumber and tomato slices. Season with salt and pepper. Spoon on cabbage mixture and top with remaining slices of buttered bread. Press together firmly. Cut sandwiches in half. To garnish, thread 4 wooden picks with tomato wedges and parsley; push into each half. Makes 2 sandwiches.

Variation: Substitute packaged shredded cabbage for red cabbage.

── Frankfurter Salad Sandwich ──

2 to 3 tablespoons potato salad
2 green onions, chopped
3 radishes, finely chopped
Salt and pepper to taste
3 tablespoons butter, softened
2 thick slices whole-wheat bread
1 teaspoon German or sweet mustard
2 frankfurters, cut diagonally in slices
8 thin cucumber slices
Green onion flowers and radish flowers
    to garnish

In a small bowl, combine potato salad, green onions and radishes. Season with salt and pepper. Mix well. Butter bread. Spread 1 slice of buttered bread with mustard. Cover with frankfurter slices. Spoon potato salad mixture over frankfurters. Smooth surface. Top with cucumber slices. Season with salt and pepper. Place remaining slice of buttered bread on top. Press together lightly. Cut diagonally in half. Garnish with green onion and radish flowers. Makes 1 sandwich.

Toasted Club Sandwich

2 large medium-thick slices white bread
1 large medium-thick slice whole-wheat
   bread
3 tablespoons butter, softened
2 ozs. sliced cooked chicken breast
1 medium-size tomato, sliced
8 thin slices cucumber
Salt and pepper to taste
1 tablespoon mayonnaise
1 hard-cooked egg, peeled, sliced
4 cocktail gherkin pickle fans and 4
   cocktail onions to garnish

Toast bread. Cut off crusts and stand upright to cool. Butter white bread on 1 side and whole-wheat bread on both sides. Cover 1 slice of buttered white bread with chicken and 1/2 of tomato and cucumber slices. Season with salt and pepper. Spread with 1/2 of mayonnaise. Top with buttered whole-wheat bread. Arrange remaining tomato and cucumber slices and egg slices on buttered whole-wheat bread. Season with salt and pepper. Spread with remaining mayonnaise. Top with remaining slice of buttered white bread. Press together firmly. Cut diagonally in triangles. To garnish, thread 4 wooden picks with pickle fans and cocktail onions; push into each triangle. Makes 1 sandwich.

Variation: Substitute sliced cheese for egg.

Four Seasons Sandwich

3 large slices whole-wheat or white bread
1 tablespoon corn oil
2 ozs. small mushrooms, cut in thick
   slices
3 tablespoons butter, softened
1 teaspoon tomato paste
1 teaspoon chopped fresh marjoram
3 slices salami, rinds removed
2 ozs. sliced mozzarella cheese
Chicory leaves
1 thick slice large tomato
Salt and pepper to taste
4 pickled chilies and additional chicory
   leaves to garnish

Toast bread. Cut off crusts and stand upright to cool. Heat oil in a small skillet. Add mushrooms and saute gently 3 minutes. Drain on paper towels and cool. In a small bowl, mix butter, tomato paste and marjoram. Spread butter mixture on 1 side of 2 slices of bread and on both sides of remaining slice of bread. Cover 1 slice of bread buttered on 1 side with salami. Add cheese. Top with chicory leaves. Cover with slice of bread buttered on both sides. Arrange mushrooms on buttered bread and top with tomato slice. Season with salt and pepper. Cover with remaining slice of buttered bread. Press together firmly. Cut diagonally in quarters. To garnish, thread 4 wooden picks with chilies and additional chicory leaves; push into each quarter. Makes 1 sandwich.

— Bacon, Lettuce & Tomato Sandwich —

8 slices bacon
4 large medium-thick slices white bread
3 tablespoons mayonnaise
4 thick slices large tomato
Salt and pepper to taste
2 crisp lettuce leaves
Sprigs of fresh parsley to garnish

In a large skillet, fry bacon until crisp. Drain on paper towels. Meanwhile, toast bread. Cut off crusts, if desired. Spread toast with mayonnaise. Arrange tomato slices on 2 slices of toast. Season with salt and pepper. Top with bacon and lettuce leaves. Cover with remaining slices of toast. Cut diagonally in quarters. Garnish with parsley. Makes 2 sandwiches.

— Double Cheese Decker Sandwich —

3 slices crusty poppy seed bread
1/3 cup butter, softened
1 tablespoon corn relish
2 ozs. Red Leicester cheese, sliced
Red bell pepper rings
2 pickled onions, sliced
1/3 bunch fresh watercress
Salt and pepper to taste
3 radicchio leaves, finely shredded
2 teaspoons French dressing
2 ozs. Emmentaler cheese, sliced

Toast bread. In a small bowl, mix butter and corn relish. Spread butter mixture on 1 side of 2 slices of toast and on both sides of remaining slice of toast. Place Red Leicester cheese on 1 slice of toast buttered on 1 side. Reserve several bell pepper rings. Top with remaining bell pepper rings and pickled onion slices. Reserve several sprigs of watercress. Cover with remaining watercress. Season with salt and pepper. Top with slice of toast buttered on both sides. In a medium-size bowl, toss shredded radicchio in dressing. Spread on buttered toast. Top with Emmentaler cheese. Cover with remaining slice of buttered toast. Press together firmly. Cut in 3 thick pieces. Garnish with reserved bell pepper rings and reserved watercress. Makes 1 sandwich.

Turkey & Ham Sandwich

3 tablespoons butter, softened
3 slices crusty seeded bread
2 to 3 ozs. sliced cooked turkey breast
Salt and pepper to taste
2 tablespoons cranberry sauce
4 small Romaine lettuce leaves
1 teaspoon mild mustard
1 tablespoon mayonnaise
2 slices cooked ham
3 radicchio leaves, finely shredded
Sprigs of fresh watercress to garnish

Butter 2 slices of bread on 1 side and remaining slice on both sides. Place turkey on 1 slice of bread buttered on 1 side. Season with salt and pepper. Spread cranberry sauce on turkey. Top with lettuce leaves. Cover with slice of bread buttered on both sides. In a small bowl, mix mustard and mayonnaise. Spread on ham. Roll up ham and cut in slices. Place on buttered bread. Top with shredded radicchio. Season with salt and pepper. Cover with remaining slice of buttered bread. Press together firmly. Cut in quarters. Garnish with watercress. Makes 1 sandwich.

Roast Beef Sandwich

2 tablespoons butter, softened
2 thick slices crusty white or whole-wheat bread
3 or 4 slices cooked rare roast beef
1 teaspoon prepared creamed horseradish
1/2 dill pickle, cut in lengthwise slices
1/2 small red onion, thinly sliced, then separated in rings
Chicory leaves
Salt and pepper to taste
2 to 3 teaspoons Thousand Island dressing
2 green onion flowers and 2 radish flowers to garnish

Butter bread. Cover 1 slice of buttered bread with roast beef, folding slices to fit bread. Spread roast beef with horseradish. Arrange dill pickle slices and onion rings over roast beef. Top with chicory leaves. Season with salt and pepper. Spread remaining slice of buttered bread with dressing. Place on chicory leaves. Press together firmly. Cut diagonally in half. Garnish with green onion flowers and radish flowers. Makes 1 sandwich.

Liverwurst & Bacon Sandwich

4 strips bacon
1/4 cup butter, softened
2 large slices whole-wheat bread
1 large slice white bread
2 ozs. liverwurst, sliced
1 tablespoon mayonnaise
6 small Belgian endive leaves
Salt and pepper to taste
Tomato relish or chili sauce
4 green bell pepper rings
Sprigs of fresh parsley to garnish

In a medium-size skillet, fry bacon until crisp. Drain on paper towels. Butter whole-wheat bread on 1 side and white bread on both sides. Arrange liverwurst on 1 slice of buttered whole-wheat bread. Spread with mayonnaise. Top with endive leaves. Season with salt and pepper. Top with buttered white bread. Spread with tomato relish. Add bell pepper rings and top with bacon. Cover with remaining slice of buttered whole-wheat bread. Press together firmly. Cut diagonally in half. Garnish with parsley sprigs. Makes 1 sandwich.

Smoked Fish Sandwich

1/2 (8-oz.) pkg. cream cheese
2 teaspoons prepared horseradish
2 teaspoons chopped fresh chives
1/4 cup butter, softened
4 thick slices crusty poppy seed bread
6 ozs. smoked mackerel, skinned, boned, flaked in large pieces
8 thin red bell pepper rings
2 teaspoons fresh lemon juice
Pepper to taste
1/3 bunch fresh watercress

In a small bowl, combine cream cheese, horseradish and chives. Butter bread. Spread 2 slices of buttered bread with cream cheese mixture. Cover with mackerel, then bell pepper rings. Sprinkle with lemon juice and season with pepper. Reserve 2 sprigs of watercress. Arrange remaining watercress on bell pepper rings. Top with remaining slices of buttered bread. Press together firmly. Cut each sandwich in half. Garnish with reserved watercress. Makes 2 sandwiches.

Variations: Substitute smoked trout or cooked, boned and skinned kippered salmon or herring for mackerel.

Pickled Herring, Onion & Egg Sandwich

4 ozs. pickled herring, drained
1 tablespoon dairy sour cream
1/2 small red onion, thinly sliced
1/4 crisp Green Delicious apple, cored,
   thinly sliced
Salt and pepper to taste
4 slices light rye bread
2 slices dark rye bread
1/4 cup butter, softened
Sprigs of fresh watercress
2 hard-cooked eggs, sliced
1/2 bunch cress
Tomato wedges to garnish

Pat pickled herring dry on paper towels. Cut in thin slivers. In a medium-size bowl, combine pickled herring slivers, sour cream, onion and apple. Season with salt and pepper. Mix well. Cut bread slices to same size, if necessary. Butter slices of light rye bread on 1 side and dark rye bread on both sides. Spread 2 slices of buttered light rye bread with pickled herring mixture. Reserve 2 sprigs of watercress. Top pickled herring mixture with remaining watercress. Cover with slices of buttered dark rye bread. Arrange egg slices on dark rye bread. Season with salt and pepper. Sprinkle liberally with cress. Top with remaining slices of buttered light rye bread. Press together firmly. Cut diagonally in half. Garnish with reserved watercress and tomato wedges. Makes 2 sandwiches.

Tuna-Avocado Sandwich

1 (3-1/2-oz.) can tuna in oil, drained
2 green onions, chopped
2 tablespoons prepared tartar sauce
Salt and pepper to taste
1 ripe avocado
1 tablespoon fresh lemon juice
1/4 cup butter, softened
4 square slices light rye bread
Small lemon wedges, additional avocado
   slices and sprigs of fresh parsley
   to garnish

Flake tuna into a medium-size bowl. Add green onions and 1 tablespoon of tartar sauce. Season with salt and pepper. Mix well. Cut avocado in half; remove pit and peel. Cut avocado in slices and dip into lemon juice. Butter bread. Cover 2 slices of buttered bread with tuna mixture and arrange avocado slices on top. Spread with remaining tartar sauce. Season with salt and pepper. Cover with remaining slices of buttered bread. Press together firmly. Cut diagonally in half. Garnish with lemon wedges, additional avocado slices and parsley. Makes 2 sandwiches.

Pork-Celery Crunch

1 tablespoon mayonnaise
1 teaspoon Dijon-style mustard
1 stalk celery, chopped
1 to 2 teaspoons applesauce, if desired
Salt and pepper to taste
2 tablespoons butter, softened
2 large thick slices whole-wheat bread
1 crisp green lettuce leaf
2 to 3 slices cooked roast pork
Red onion rings
Celery leaves to garnish

In a small bowl, mix mayonnaise, mustard, celery and applesauce, if desired.

Season with salt and pepper. Mix well. Butter bread. Place lettuce leaf on 1 slice of buttered bread. Add pork and spoon celery mixture over pork. Reserve several red onion rings. Cover celery mixture with remaining red onion rings. Top with remaining slice of buttered bread. Press together lightly. Cut diagonally in quarters. Garnish with reserved red onion rings and celery leaves. Makes 1 sandwich.

Variation: Substitute cold roast beef or corned beef for pork and applesauce.

Peanut-Banana Sandwich

3 thin slices whole-wheat bread
2 tablespoon crunchy peanut butter
1 banana
1 tablespoon fresh lemon juice
1/4 to 1/2 teaspoon ground cinnamon
1 teaspoon soft light-brown sugar
2 ozs. cream cheese, softened
1/4 Red or Green Delicious apple, cored, to decorate

Spread 1 slice of bread with 1 tablespoon of peanut butter. Cut 2 slices from banana; dip into lemon juice. Reserve for decoration. Cut remaining banana in half crosswise, then in thin lengthwise slices. Dip into lemon juice. In a small bowl, mix cinnamon and brown sugar. Cover peanut butter with

1/2 of banana slices. Sprinkle with a small amount of brown sugar mixture. Spread 1 slice of bread with cream cheese. Place, cheese-side down, over sliced banana. Spread with remaining peanut butter and cover with remaining banana slices. Sprinkle with a small amount of brown sugar mixture. Spread remaining slice of bread with remaining cream cheese and place over banana slices. Press together firmly. Cut diagonally in half. Cut apple in 2 wedges. Dip into lemon juice. To decorate, thread reserved banana slices and apple wedges onto wooden picks. Sprinkle with remaining brown sugar mixture; push into each half. Makes 1 sandwich.

Chicken Maryland Rolls

4 crusty poppy seed bowknot-shaped
  rolls
1/3 cup butter, softened
2 (4-oz.) skinned boneless chicken breasts
Salt and pepper to taste
1/2 cup all-purpose flour
1 egg
1 tablespoon milk
2 green onions, chopped
2 baking potatoes, grated
1/4 cup canned or frozen corn, thawed
  if frozen
Vegetable oil for shallow frying
2 small bananas
Green leaf lettuce leaves
Tomato relish
2 tomatoes, thinly sliced
Fresh cress to garnish

Cut rolls in half. Spread with 1/4 cup of butter. Cut each chicken breast in 4 thin slices, cutting at an angle. Season with salt and pepper. In a large bowl, mix flour, egg and milk. Add green onions, potatoes and corn. Season with salt and pepper. Mix well. Heat oil in a large skillet. Divide potato mixture in 4 equal portions. Press in patties the same size as rolls. Fry patties 6 minutes or until golden, turning once. Drain on paper towels and keep warm. Pour oil from skillet. Heat remaining butter in skillet. Fry chicken slices 2 to 3 minutes on each side. Drain on paper towels and keep warm. Cut bananas in half crosswise and then in half lengthwise. Fry in skillet 30 to 45 seconds. Spread tomato relish on rolls, then top with lettuce leaves. Place potato patties on lettuce leaves. Add tomatoes, chicken and bananas. Cover with top halves of rolls. Secure with wooden picks. Garnish with cress. Makes 4 rolls.

Smoked Salmon Bagels

2 plain bagels
2 (3-oz.) pkgs. cream cheese
2 teaspoons fresh lemon juice
2 tablespoons dairy sour cream
3 green onions, chopped
Dash cayenne pepper
2 to 3 ozs. thinly sliced smoked salmon
Green onion flowers and lemon twists to
  garnish

Preheat oven to 350F (175C). Wrap bagels in foil. Heat in preheated oven 15 minutes. Meanwhile, in a medium-size bowl, combine cream cheese, lemon juice, sour cream, green onions and cayenne pepper. Roll smoked salmon in rolls; cut in thin slices. Cut warmed bagels in half. Spread each cut side with 1/2 of cream cheese mixture. Arrange salmon slices on bottom halves of bagels. Cover with top halves. Garnish with green onion flowers and lemon twists. Makes 2 bagels.

Brie & Fig Tempter

1-1/2 teaspoons unsalted butter, softened
1 rye crispbread or Scandinavian
   flatbread
2 or 3 small red leaf lettuce leaves
3 thin slices Brie cheese
1 fresh ripe fig, cut in 6 wedges
1 teaspoon fresh lime juice
Lime twists to garnish

Butter crispbread. Cover with lettuce leaves. Press down lightly. Arrange overlapping slices of cheese at a slight angle over lettuce leaves allowing ends to slightly overlap edges. Sprinkle fig wedges with lime juice. Arrange attractively with cheese. Garnish with lime twists. Makes 1 sandwich.

Variation: Substitute light or dark rye bread, sliced diagonally, for crispbread. Substitute sliced kiwifruit for fig.

Egg & Anchovy Salad Sandwich

1-1/2 teaspoons unsalted butter, softened
1 slice crusty poppy seed bread
2 ozs. cream cheese, softened
1 tablespoon mayonnaise
1/2 teaspoon tomato paste
Salt and pepper to taste
1 small green leaf lettuce leaf
1 hard-boiled egg, peeled, sliced
5 or 6 anchovy fillets, drained, patted
   dry, rolled
6 or 7 thin red bell pepper strips
Paprika
Sprigs of fresh watercress to garnish

Butter bread. In a small bowl, mix cream cheese, mayonnaise and tomato paste until soft and well combined. Season with salt and pepper. Mix well. Spoon 3/4 of cream cheese mixture into lettuce leaf. Spread remainder over buttered bread. Arrange overlapping egg slices over crusty top and down 1 side of buttered bread. Place filled lettuce leaf in remaining space. Arrange rolled anchovy fillets around edge of cream cheese mixture in lettuce leaf. Place bell pepper strips around edge of each egg slice. Sprinkle paprika on cream cheese mixture. Garnish with watercress. Makes 1 sandwich.

Tongue Petal Salad Sandwich

1-1/2 teaspoons unsalted butter, softened
1 slice pumpernickel bread
Sprigs of fresh dill
1 slice cooked beef tongue
3 thin slices cucumber
3 slices tomato
1-1/2 tablespoons coleslaw
Radish flowers to garnish

Butter bread. Reserve 2 sprigs of dill. Cover edges of bread with remaining dill allowing dill to overlap edges of bread. Using a 2-inch round cutter, cut 3 rounds from beef tongue. Arrange overlapping rounds of tongue in a petal-like design over bread. Place cucumber and tomato slices between tongue rounds to give an attractive "flower" pattern. Spoon coleslaw into center. Garnish with reserved sprigs of dill and radish flowers. Makes 1 sandwich.

Variation: Substitute any cooked cold meat, such as ham, salami or bologna, for cooked tongue. Substitute thin slices of kiwifruit for cucumber and top with Waldorf salad or potato salad instead of coleslaw.

Ham & Asparagus Special

6 frozen asparagus spears
1-1/2 teaspoons unsalted butter, softened
1 slice pumpernickel bread
1/4 bunch cress
2 slices cooked ham
1 small tomato, cut in wedges
Mayonnaise and paprika to garnish

Cook asparagus spears following package directions. Drain, pat dry on paper towels and cool. Butter bread. Arrange cress around edges of bread. Cut ham in 2 (3-inch) squares. Place 3 asparagus spears diagonally across each square of ham. Trim stalks, if necessary. Fold sides to middle. Secure with wooden picks. Arrange ham and asparagus "envelopes" at an angle over buttered bread. Add tomato wedges. Garnish with piped mayonnaise and sprinkle with paprika. Makes 1 sandwich.

Note: Canned asparagus spears may be used, although the color is not as bright.

Mango & Crab Sandwich

1-1/2 teaspoons unsalted butter, softened
1 slice dark rye bread, cut diagonally
   in half
2 ozs. white crabmeat
1 green onion, finely chopped
3 tablespoon mayonnaise
3 drops hot-pepper sauce
Few drops fresh lemon juice
Salt and pepper to taste
Chicory leaves
1/2 small ripe mango, pitted, peeled, cut
   in thin slivers
1 or 2 green onion flowers and lemon
   slices, cut in quarters, to garnish

Butter bread. Flake crabmeat into a small bowl. Add green onion, 2 teaspoons of mayonnaise, hot-pepper sauce and lemon juice to flaked crabmeat. Season with salt and pepper. Mix well. Cover buttered bread with chicory leaves. Spoon crab mixture onto center of chicory leaves. Arrange mango around crab mixture. In a pastry bag fitted with a small star tube, pipe a rosette with remaining mayonnaise on 2 opposite corners of sandwich. Garnish with green onion flowers and lemon slices. Makes 1 sandwich.

Spiced Egg Slice

1 hard-cooked egg, peeled, chopped
1 tablespoon mayonnaise
1 oz. Cheddar cheese, finely diced
1 green onion, chopped
1/2 to 3/4 teaspoon concentrated curry
   paste or 1 teaspoon curry powder
   plus 1 teaspoon mayonnaise
Salt and pepper to taste
1-1/2 teaspoons butter, softened
1 slice pumpernickel bread
16 thin cucumber slices
2 radish flowers and sprigs of fresh mint
   to garnish

In a small bowl, mix hard-cooked egg, mayonnaise, Cheddar cheese, green onion and curry paste. Season with salt and pepper. Butter bread. Arrange overlapping slices of cucumber around edge of buttered bread, allowing slices to slightly overlap edges of bread. Spoon curried egg mixture into center. Smooth slightly to cover inner edges of cucumber slices. Garnish with radish flowers and mint. Makes 1 sandwich.

Variation: Substitute dairy sour cream for mayonnaise and 1 tablespoon chopped chives for green onion.

Ham & Pineapple Muffins

2 plain muffins, cut in half
2 tablespoons butter
4 (1/4-inch-thick) slices cooked ham
4 thick slices large tomato
4 canned pineapple slices, drained
1 tablespoon plus 1 teaspoon piccalilli or
   hot dog relish
1 cup grated Jarlsberg cheese
1/2 cup grated red-veined Cheddar
   cheese
Sprigs of fresh cilantro to garnish

Preheat broiler. Toast muffins. Spread with butter. Using a 3-1/2-inch round cutter, cut 4 rounds from slices of ham. Preheat broiler. Place ham rounds on buttered muffins. Top with tomato slices. Pat pineapple slices dry on paper towels; place on tomato slices. Spoon piccalilli into each pineapple center. In a small bowl, combine cheeses. Mound on pineapple. Broil under preheated broiler 6 to 7 minutes or until cheese is melted, bubbling and light golden. Garnish with cilantro. Makes 4 muffins.

Beef & Endive Crunch

1-1/2 teaspoons unsalted butter, softened
1 slice pumpernickel bread
4 or 5 Belgian endive leaves
1 teaspoon mayonnaise
1 teaspoon prepared creamed
   horseradish
2 slices cooked rare roast beef
1 tablespoon pickled red cabbage,
   drained
Sprigs of fresh dill and cucumber twists
   to garnish

Butter bread. Arrange endive leaves at an angle over buttered bread. In a small bowl, mix mayonnaise and creamed horseradish. Spread on slices of beef. Fold beef slices and place on endive leaves. Spoon on red cabbage. Garnish with dill and cucumber twists. Makes 1 sandwich.

Variation: Substitute slices of cooked ham or tongue for rare roast beef. Substitute shredded radicchio leaves, tossed in French dressing, for pickled red cabbage.

Italian Special

1-1/2 teaspoons unsalted butter, softened
1 slice light or dark rye bread, cut
    diagonally in half
2 or 3 small red or green leaf lettuce
    leaves
2 slices prosciutto
2 or 3 thin slices mozzarella cheese
2 or 3 tomato slices
2 or 3 pitted black or green olives
1/2 teaspoon olive oil
1/2 teaspoon chopped fresh basil
Freshly ground pepper to taste
Sprigs of fresh basil to garnish

Butter bread. Cover buttered bread with lettuce leaves. Roll proscuitto in cone shaped rolls. Place rolls slightly to 1 side at a slight angle over lettuce leaves. Arrange an overlapping border of alternating cheese and tomato slices in front of rolls. Place olives in center of rolls. Drizzle olive oil over cheese and tomato slices, then sprinkle with chopped basil. Season with pepper. Garnish with sprigs of basil. Makes 1 sandwich.

Variation: Substitute slices of salami, mortadella or bologna cut in half for prosciutto.

Potted Shrimp Treat

3 tablespoons plus 1-1/2 teaspoons
    unsalted butter
2 ozs. peeled fresh shrimp, coarsely
    chopped
1/2 small clove garlic, crushed
1/8 teaspoon ground cumin
1/8 teaspoon ground mace
1/8 teaspoon cayenne pepper
1 teaspoon finely chopped fresh parsley
Salt and white pepper to taste
1 slice pumpernickel bread
3 or 4 small radicchio leaves
Sprigs of fresh flat-leafed parsley
1 peeled cooked shrimp to garnish

In a small saucepan, melt 1 tablespoon of butter. Add chopped shrimp and garlic. Cook gently 1 minute. Remove from heat and stir in cumin, mace, cayenne pepper and chopped parsley. Season with salt and white pepper. Mix well. Spoon mixture into a 1/2-cup ramekin. Smooth surface. Wash saucepan. Melt 2 tablespoons of butter in saucepan. Cool slightly, then pour over shrimp mixture. Cool and refrigerate 2 hours or until set. Spread remaining butter over bread. Top with radicchio leaves. Run a knife around edge of ramekin to loosen shrimp mold. Invert and remove shrimp mold. Place in center of bread. Arrange parsley around mold. Garnish with peeled shrimp. Makes 1 sandwich.

Roquefort Grape Relish Sandwich

1-1/2 teaspoons unsalted butter, softened
1 slice dark rye bread, cut diagonally in half
Green lettuce leaves
2 or 3 slices Roquefort cheese
2 or 3 sprigs seedless black or green grapes
2 teaspoons dairy sour cream
Lime twists and sprigs of fresh chervil to garnish

Butter bread. Cover buttered bread with lettuce leaves allowing tips of leaves to overlap edges of bread. Arrange overlapping slices of cheese over lettuce. Place grapes on 1 side and spoon sour cream on other side. Garnish with lime twists and chervil. Makes 1 sandwich.

Variation: Substitute Gorgonzolia cheese for Roquefort cheese and sprigs of watercress for green lettuce leaves. Substitute mayonnaise for dairy sour cream.

Gravlax Slice

1-1/2 teaspoons unsalted butter, softened
1 slice light rye bread, cut diagonally in half
12 large watercress leaves
2 ozs. sliced Gravlax
3 cucumber twists
2 teaspoons dairy sour cream
1/2 teaspoon wholegrain mustard
Sprigs of fresh dill to garnish

Butter bread. Arrange watercress leaves around edge of buttered bread to form a border, allowing leaves to overlap edges of bread. Arrange slices of Gravlax over buttered bread. Place cucumber twists across 1 end. In a small bowl, mix sour cream and mustard. Spoon onto sandwich in a swirl. Garnish with dill. Makes 1 sandwich.

Variation: Substitute thinly sliced smoked salmon, rolled, for Gravlax. Garnish with lemon wedges, fresh chervil and black lumpfish caviar.

Note: Gravlax is pickled fresh salmon flavored with dill. It is now widely available, fresh or frozen, from delicatessens and specialty food markets.

Danish Herring on Rye

1-1/2 teaspoons unsalted butter, softened
1 slice light or dark rye bread, cut
    diagonally in half
3 or 4 small Romaine lettuce leaves
Salt and pepper to taste
2 ozs. pickled herring, drained
1/4 crisp Red Delicious apple, cored,
    thinly sliced
2 teaspoons lemon juice
Small onion rings, lemon twist and
    sprigs of fresh dill to garnish

Butter bread. Arrange lettuce leaves diagonally on buttered bread allowing
leaf tips to overlap edges of bread. Press
leaves down firmly in center to flatten
slightly. Season with salt and pepper.
Place pickled herring in center. Brush
apple slices with lemon juice and arrange around pickled herring. Garnish
with onion rings, lemon twist and dill.
Makes 1 sandwich.

Variation: Substitute thin slivers of red
and green bell pepper for apples.

Stilton-Pear Topper

1-1/2 teaspoons unsalted butter, softened
1 slice crusty whole-wheat bread
Chicory leaves
2 slices Stilton cheese
1/2 ripe pear, cored, sliced
1 teaspoon lemon juice
1 large walnut half
Lemon twist and sprigs of fresh
    watercress to garnish

Butter bread. Place chicory leaves on
buttered bread. Press down lightly.
Place cheese on top of bread. Brush
pear slices with lemon juice; arrange in
an overlapping fan-shape on 1 side of
cheese. Add walnut half. Garnish with
lemon twist and watercress. Makes 1
sandwich.

Variation: Substitute Danish Blue,
Cambozola, Dolcelatte or Roquefort
cheese for Stilton cheese. Substitute
star fruit slices for pear slices.

Goujons of Plaice Tartare

1 flounder fillet, skinned, boned, cut in
    very thin strips
1 teaspoon all-purpose flour
Salt and pepper to taste
1 small egg, beaten
2 to 3 tablespoons dry bread crumbs
Vegetable oil for frying
1-1/2 teaspoons unsalted butter, softened
1 slice dark rye bread, cut diagonally in
    half
1 large crisp lettuce leaf
4 red bell pepper rings
1/2 teaspoon lemon juice
Small lemon wedges and sprigs of fresh
    parsley to garnish
1 tablespoon prepared tartar sauce

Coat fish strips with flour. Season with
salt and pepper. Dip strips into beaten
egg. Coat in bread crumbs. Heat oil in a
small skillet. Fry fish strips 2 to 3 minutes or until golden brown and cooked
through. Drain on paper towels and
cool. Butter bread. Place lettuce leaf on
buttered bread. Arrange bell pepper
rings over lettuce. Mound fish strips on
top. Season with salt and pepper.
Sprinkle with lemon juice. If desired,
cut in half diagonally. Garnish with
lemon wedges and parsley. Serve with
tartar sauce. Makes 1 sandwich.

Savory Boats

4 (1-inch-thick) slices white bread, crusts
    removed
Vegetable oil for frying
3 hard-cooked eggs, peeled
1-1/2 to 2 tablespoons salad dresing
Salt and pepper to taste
1/2 bunch cress
2 slices processed Cheddar cheese, room
    temperature
8 thin slices cucumber
4 cherry tomatoes, cut in half
Finely shredded green lettuce

Cut slices of bread in half crosswise. Cut
off ends diagonally to form boat-
shapes. Heat oil in a large skillet. Fry
bread until golden brown on both sides.
Drain on paper towels and cool. In a
small bowl, mash eggs finely and mix
with salad dressing. Season with salt

and pepper. Mix well. Pile mixture onto
fried bread boats. Using a knife,
smooth sides to same shape as boats.
Remove green leaves from cress. Press
cress leaves onto sides of egg mixture to
coat evenly. To make sails, cut cheese
diagonally in quarters. Thread cheese
and cucumber slices onto 8 wooden
picks. Secure cherry tomato halves to
top of wooden picks; push into centers
of boats. Arrange boats on a bed of
lettuce. Makes 8 pieces.

Variation: Substitute chopped salted
peanuts for cress. Substitute drained
canned salmon for egg. Flake salmon
finely and mix with half and half or
vinegar. Season to taste with salt and
pepper. Substitute whole-wheat bread
for white bread.

Ham & Cheese Boats

3 large slices white or whole-wheat
    bread, crusts removed
1-1/2 tablespoons olive oil
1 garlic clove, crushed
1/4 cup finely chopped cooked ham
1/2 cup shredded Cheddar cheese
1 tablespoon tomato paste
1 tablespoon mayonnaise
1 teaspoon chopped fresh marjoram
Salt and pepper to taste
1 (2-oz.) can anchovy fillets, drained
3 stuffed olives, sliced, and sprigs of
    fresh marjoram to garnish

Preheat oven to 375F (190C). Using a
rolling pin, firmly roll slices of bread to
flatten. In a 1-cup measure, mix oil and
garlic. Brush over both sides of each
slice of bread. Cut slices in half lengthwise. Line 6 (3-3/4" x 2") boat-shaped

pans. Press oiled bread into pans firmly
by pressing another pan on top of oiled
bread. Trim edges with scissors. Place
bread-lined pans on a baking sheet. In a
small bowl, mix ham, cheese, tomato
paste, mayonnaise and chopped marjoram. Season with salt and pepper.
Mix well. Spoon mixture into pans. Using flat side of a knife, flatten surfaces.
Cut anchovy fillets in half lengthwise
and then in half crosswise. Arrange 4
pieces on each ham mixture in a lattice
design. Bake in preheated oven 20 to
25 minutes or until golden and cooked
through. Cool in pans 5 minutes. Invert
and carefully remove boats. Garnish
center of each boat with stuffed olive
slices and a sprig of marjoram. Serve
warm. Makes 6 boats.

Saucisson en Brioche

1 (1/4-oz.) pkg. active dry yeast (about 1
    tablespoon)
2 teaspoons sugar
1/4 cup warm water (110F/45C)
2 cups bread flour
1/4 teaspoon salt
2 large eggs, beaten
1/4 cup butter, melted
1 (7- to 8-oz.) piece cooked beef sausage,
    about 2 inches wide and 7 inches long
1-1/2 tablespoons chopped fresh parsley
1 egg yolk, beaten
Sprigs of fresh parsley to garnish

Grease a large bowl. In a small bowl,
blend yeast, sugar and water. Let stand
until foamy. In a large bowl, combine
flour and salt. Add yeast liquid, eggs
and butter. Mix to a soft dough. Turn
out dough onto a lightly floured surface. Knead 5 minutes or until firm. Put
dough in greased bowl and cover with
oiled plastic wrap. Let stand in a warm

place until doubled in size, about 1
hour. Oil an 8-1/2" x 4-1/2" loaf pan.
Knead dough on a floured surface. Using a rolling pin, roll dough to a 9" x 7"
rectangle. Place sausage lengthwise on
longside of dough. Sprinkle sausage
with chopped parsley. Wrap sausage in
dough, overlapping dough on bottom.
Dampen edges and seal well. Put roll,
seam-side down, in pan. Pierce 3 holes
through to sausage along top of dough.
Put a roll of greased foil in each hole.
Cover with oiled plastic wrap. Let stand
in a warm place until dough reaches top
of pan, about 45 minutes. Meanwhile,
preheat oven to 375F (190C). Brush
top of loaf with egg yolk. Bake in preheated oven 30 to 35 minutes or until
golden. If necessary, cover with foil
during baking to prevent overbrown-
ing. Slice, garnish with parsley sprigs
and serve hot. Makes 6 to 8 pieces.

Pâté Salad Croissants

2 croissants
2 tablespoons butter, softened
1-1/2 ozs. Boursin cheese
6 small Romaine lettuce leaves
2 thick slices large tomato, cut in half
4 ozs. firm pâté, sliced
Salt and pepper to taste
2 crisp bacon rolls, 2 pitted black olives
   and 2 small lettuce leaves to garnish

Cut croissants 2/3 way through center, cutting from rounded side through to pointed side; do not cut through crust. Open slightly and spread both sides of each croissant lightly with butter.

Spread 1 side of each croissant with cheese. Place lettuce leaves at an angle. Add half a tomato slice to each croissant. Arrange slices of pâté along 1 side of each croissant. Place remaining halved tomato slices along other side of pâté. Season with salt and pepper. To garnish, thread 2 wooden picks with bacon rolls, black olives and lettuce leaves; push into each croissant. Makes 2 croissants.

Variation: Top filled croissants with a small amount of mayonnaise or pickle.

Salmon & Egg Croissants

2 croissants
3 eggs
3 tablespoons whipping cream
Pepper to taste
3 ozs. smoked salmon, chopped
1/2 cup grated Cheddar cheese
2 teaspoons chopped fresh parsley
1 tablespoon butter
Sprigs of fresh Italian parsley to garnish

Cut croissants 2/3 way through center, cutting from rounded side through to pointed sides; do not cut through crust. Warm croissants. Meanwhile, in a small bowl, beat eggs and cream. Season with pepper. Mix well. Stir in smoked salmon, cheese and chopped parsley. Melt butter in a medium-size nonstick skillet. Pour in egg mixture. Cook over a medium heat until just set and cooked through, stirring constantly. Open croissant and spoon in egg mixture. Garnish with parsley sprigs. Serve at once. Makes 2 croissants.

Traffic Lights

2 large slices whole-wheat bread, crusts removed
2 large slices white bread, crusts removed
1/4 cup butter, softened
2 teaspoons Thousand Island dressing
2 green lettuce leaves, finely shredded
2 hard-cooked eggs, peeled, sliced
5 slices tomato
Salt and pepper to taste
Green onion flowers to garnish

Butter bread. Spread whole-wheat slices of buttered bread with Thousand Island dressing. Reserve a small amount of lettuce. Cover 1/3 of each slice of whole-wheat bread with remaining lettuce. Remove egg yolks from whites. Reserve several slices of egg yolk. Arrange yolk slices over center of lettuce. Place 2 slices of tomato over remaining area of each slice of bread. Season with salt and pepper. Using a small 3/4-inch plain or fluted round cutter, cut out 6 rounds from each slice of buttered white bread. Reserve bread rounds for another use. Place slices of buttered bread over tomatoes. Press together firmly. Cut each sandwich in half to form traffic lights. Chop reserved lettuce, slices of egg yolk and remaining slice of tomato. Fill relevant holes in sandwich. Garnish with green onion flowers. Makes 2 sandwiches.

Variation: Substitute shredded Cheddar cheese for hard-cooked egg.

Party Sandwich Cake

1 large loaf whole-wheat or white uncut sandwich bread, crusts removed
1/3 cup butter, softened
1 (8-oz.) and 2 (3-oz.) packages cream cheese, softened
1-1/2 tablespoons prepared coleslaw, finely chopped
1 green onion, finely chopped
1/4 bunch cress
1 (3-1/2-oz.) can salmon, drained
2 teaspoons mayonnaise
1 teaspoon tomato paste
Salt and pepper to taste
2 ozs. Cambozola cheese or other blue cheese, sliced
2 tablespoons chopped red bell pepper
1 tablespoon plus 1 teaspoon milk
3/4 cup toasted almonds, finely chopped
3 tablespoons black lumpfish caviar or chopped chives and sprigs of fresh mint to garnish

Cut bread lengthwise in 4 slices. Butter bottom and top slices on 1 side and remaining slices on both sides. In a medium-size bowl, blend 2 ounces of cream cheese, coleslaw and green onion. Spread on bottom slice of buttered bread. Sprinkle with cress. Top with a slice of bread buttered on both sides. In a small bowl, combine salmon, mayonnaise and tomato paste. Season with salt and pepper. Mix well. Spread on buttered bread. Cover with another slice of bread buttered on both sides. Place slices of cheese on buttered bread. Sprinkle with bell pepper. Cover with top slice of buttered bread. In a small bowl, beat remaining cream cheese and milk until soft. Spread over top and sides of cake. Reserve 2 tablespoons of almonds. Coat all 4 sides with remaining almonds. Mark top of cake in 1-inch diagonal rows. Fill alternate rows with reserved almonds and lumpfish caviar. Garnish with mint. Slice and cut in fingers. Makes 30 pieces.

Cheese-Cress Pinwheels

3 (1/4-inch) lengthwise slices uncut
    whole-wheat bread, crusts removed
3 tablespoons butter, softened
2 (3-oz.) packages cream cheese
2 teaspoons half and half
1 bunch watercress, stalks trimmed, then
    finely chopped
1 garlic clove, crushed
1-1/2 whole pimentoes, drained
Radish flowers and sprigs of fresh
    watercress to garnish

Using a rolling pin, firmly roll each slice
of bread to flatten. Butter flattened
bread. In a small bowl, mix cream
cheese, half and half, watercress and
garlic until soft and well combined.

Spread cream cheese mixture on buttered bread. Pat pimento dry on paper
towels. Cut in thin strips. Arrange
crosswise down length of bread. Roll
up, jelly-roll style, starting from a short
side. Wrap individually in plastic wrap.
Refrigerate at least 2 hours. Remove
plastic wrap. Cut each roll in 8 pinwheels. Arrange on a serving plate.
Garnish with radish flowers and watercress. Makes 24 pinwheels.

Variations: Tint cream cheese mixture
pink with a small amount of tomato
paste. Substitute white bread for whole-
wheat bread.

Salmon Pinwheels

2 (1/4-inch-thick) lengthwise slices white
    uncut sandwich bread,
    crusts removed
1/3 cup butter, softened
3 tablespoons finely chopped fresh
    parsley
1 teaspoon fresh lemon juice
1/8 teaspoon cayenne pepper
4 ozs. thinly sliced smoked salmon
Pepper to taste
Lemon twists and sprigs of fresh parsley
    to garnish

Using a rolling pin, roll each slice of
bread firmly to flatten. In a small bowl,
combine butter, 1 tablespoon of
chopped parsley, lemon juice and

cayenne pepper. Spread 2/3 of butter
mixture on flattened bread. Arrange
slices of salmon on buttered bread and
season with pepper. Roll up each slice,
jelly-roll style, starting from a short
side. Spread remaining butter on outside of rolls and coat evenly in remaining chopped parsley. Wrap rolls tightly
in plastic wrap. Chill at least 2 hours.
Remove plastic wrap. Cut each roll in 7
slices. Garnish with lemon twists and
parsley sprigs. Makes 14 pieces.

Variation: Coat 1 buttered roll with
chopped parsley and the other roll in
paprika. Chill and cut in slices.

Sesame Shrimp Fingers

4 ozs. fresh or frozen peeled cooked shrimp, thawed if frozen, coarsely chopped
1 (1/2-inch) piece gingerroot, peeled, grated
1 garlic clove, crushed
2 teaspoons light soy sauce
1 tablespoon ketchup
2 green onions, chopped
Pepper to taste
1/4 cup butter, softened
4 medium-thick slices white or whole-wheat bread, crusts removed
2 eggs, beaten
2 tablespoons milk
2 tablespoons sesame seeds
1 tablespoon corn oil
Unpeeled cooked shrimp, sprigs of fresh cilantro and slivers of green onion to garnish

In a medium-size bowl, combine shrimp, gingerroot, garlic, soy sauce, ketchup and chopped green onions. Season with pepper. Mix well. Butter bread with 1/2 of butter. Spread shrimp mixture on 2 slices of buttered bread. Cover with remaining slices of buttered bread. Press together firmly. In a small bowl, beat eggs and milk. Pour into a shallow dish. Dip sandwiches into egg mixture until well soaked. Sprinkle both sides with sesame seeds. Heat remaining butter and oil in a medium-size skillet. Fry sandwiches 5 to 6 minutes or until golden, turning occasionally. Cut each sandwich in 3 fingers. Garnish with unpeeled shrimp, cilantro and green onion slivers. Serve hot. Makes 2 sandwiches.

Piquant Salmon Treats

6 ozs. salmon steak
1 teaspoon fresh lemon juice
Salt and pepper to taste
1 to 2 teaspoons capers, drained
3 tablespoons mayonnaise
3 cocktail gherkin pickles, chopped
1 green onion, chopped
2 (1/4-inch-thick) lengthwise slices uncut white sandwich bread, crusts removed
3 tablespoons butter, softened
Paprika
Sprigs of fresh parsley to garnish

Preheat oven to 350F (175C). Butter a sheet of foil large enough to enclose salmon. Place salmon on buttered foil. Sprinkle with lemon juice and season with salt and pepper. Wrap foil to enclose salmon. Place on a baking sheet. Bake in preheated oven 25 minutes. Cool, then skin and bone salmon. Flake salmon into a medium-size bowl. Dry capers on paper towels and chop finely. Add capers, mayonnaise, pickles and green onion to salmon. Season with salt and pepper. Mix well. Using a rolling pin, lightly roll bread to flatten slightly. Butter 1 slice on 1 side and remaining slice on both sides. Using 2-inch fluted round cutter, cut 8 rounds from bread buttered on 1 side. Cover bread rounds with salmon mixture, reserving a small amount. Using same cutter, cut 8 rounds from remaining bread buttered on both sides. Using a 3/4-inch fluted round cutter, cut centers from bread rounds and discard centers. Sprinkle bread rounds with paprika and place on salmon. Press together lightly. Spoon reserved salmon mixture into centers. Garnish with parsley. Makes 8 pieces.

Mini Rye Clubs

4 slices pumpernickel bread
2 thin slices light rye bread
1/4 cup butter, softened
4 thin slices cooked beef tongue or ham
1/2 teaspoon Dijon-style mustard
2 small tomatoes, thinly sliced
Salt and pepper to taste
Fresh sprigs of watercress
2 ozs. Dolcelatte or other blue cheese cheese, softened
2 teaspoons mayonnaise
3 tablespoons finely chopped fresh chives
8 stuffed green olives to garnish

Using a 3-inch plain round cutter, cut 4 rounds from slices of pumpernickel bread and 2 rounds from slices of light rye bread. Butter pumpernickel bread rounds on 1 side and light rye bread rounds on both sides. Using same cutter, cut 4 rounds from slices of tongue. Spread 2 tongue rounds with mustard and sandwich together in pairs. Arrange slices of tomato over 2 pumpernickel bread rounds. Season with salt and pepper. Cover each with a pair of tongue rounds. Top with light rye bread rounds and cover with watercress. Spread cheese over buttered sides of remaining pumpernickel bread rounds. Place cheese-sides down over watercress. Press together firmly. Cut in quarters. Secure each piece with a wooden pick. Spread a straight edge of each piece with mayonnaise. Using a knife, press chopped chives onto mayonnaise to coat evenly. To garnish, thread olives on 8 wooden picks; push into each quarter. Makes 8 pieces.

Celery-Pâté Sticks

4 ozs. soft smooth pâté
1/2 (8-oz.) package cream cheese, softened
Few drops hot-pepper sauce
2 slices pumpernickel bread, crusts removed
1 tablespoon butter, softened
2 stalks celery
2 radishes, sliced, and sprigs of fresh parsley to garnish

In a medium-size bowl, mix pâté, cream cheese and hot-pepper sauce until soft and well combined. Cut each slice of bread in 4 (1-1/2-inch) squares. Spread lightly with butter. Cut celery in 8 (1-1/4-inch) lengths. In a pastry bag fitted with a small star tube, pipe pâté mixture in a diagonal design on buttered bread and down middle of celery. Arrange celery diagonally over decorated bread. Cut slices of radishes in quarters. Arrange 2 pieces on each side of celery and 3 pieces on pâté in celery. Add 2 small parsley sprigs to 2 opposite corners. Makes 8 pieces.

Variation: Substitute mini-toasts (crisp golden squares of toast sold in packets of about 33) for pumpernickel bread.

Glazed Chicken Canapés

1/3 cup butter
3 tablespoons all-purpose flour
1-1/4 cups milk
Salt and white pepper to taste
2 (1/4-oz.) envelopes unflavored gelatin
1-1/4 cups boiling chicken stock
4 to 6 (1/4-inch-thick) slices cooked
    chicken breast
1 whole canned pimento, drained
Cucumber skin
Sprigs of fresh parsley
8 slices pumpernickel bread
1/2 cup chopped pistachio nuts
Sprigs of fresh chervil to garnish

To prepare sauce, melt 2 tablespoons of butter in a medium-size saucepan. Stir in flour; cook 1 minute, stirring constantly. Add milk and bring to a boil. Simmer 2 minutes, stirring constantly. Season with salt and pepper. Mix well. Prepare gelatin according to directions, using chicken stock for liq-

uid. Stir 1/2 of gelatin into warm sauce. Stir well, then pour through a sieve into a medium-size bowl. Using a 1-1/2-inch plain cutter, cut slices of chicken in 15 to 20 rounds. Place chicken rounds on a wire rack set over a plate. Coat with sauce, allowing excess to run off. Let stand 15 minutes. To decorate, pat pimento dry on a paper towel. Using an aspic cutter, cut pimento in flowers. Cut cucumber skin in leaf shapes and parsley stalks in stems. Dip decorations into gelatin and arrange on top to form "flowers." Let stand 15 minutes or until set. Spoon gelatin over "flowers" to glaze. Let stand 30 minutes. Using 1-1/2-inch plain cutter, cut bread in 15 to 20 rounds. Spread tops and edges with remaining butter and dip edges into nuts. Place decorated chicken rounds on buttered bread rounds. Garnish with chervil. Makes 15 to 20 pieces.

Anchovy Mosaics

1/4 cup butter, softened
1-1/4 teaspoons fresh lemon juice
1/2 (2-oz.) can anchovy fillets, drained,
    very finely chopped
1 cocktail gherkin pickle, finely chopped
1 teaspoon capers, well drained, finely
    chopped
1/2 to 1 teaspoon finely chopped fresh
    marjoram
1/2 teaspoon Thousand Island dressing
2 large thin slices whole-wheat bread
2 large thin slices white bread
2 or 3 (1/4-inch-thick) slices avocado
1 canned whole pimento, well drained,
    patted dry
Sprigs of fresh marjoram to garnish

In a small bowl, mix 2 tablespoons of butter, 1/4 teaspoon of lemon juice, anchovies, pickle, capers, finely chopped marjoram and dressing until well combined. Spread mixture on whole-wheat bread. Using a 2-inch fluted round cutter, cut out 4 rounds from each slice of buttered white bread. Using a small 1-inch star-shaped cutter, cut out centers of white bread rounds and discard. Place buttered rounds of white bread, buttered-sides down, over whole-wheat bread rounds. Press together lightly. Dip avocado slices in remaining lemon juice. Using 1-inch star-shaped cutter, cut out 4 stars from avocado slices and pimento. Place avocado and pimento stars on white bread. Garnish with sprigs of marjoram. Makes 8 pieces.

Hot Shrimp Rolls

4 large medium-thick slices white bread, crusts removed
1 tablespoon butter, softened
2 tablespoons all-purpose flour
1/3 cup milk
2 teaspoons freshly grated Parmesan cheese
Finely grated peel 1/2 lemon
3 ozs. peeled cooked fresh or frozen shrimp, thawed if frozen, chopped
1 tablespoon chopped fresh parsley
Salt and pepper to taste
Vegetable oil for deep frying
1 egg, beaten
3 tablespoons dry bread crumbs
Lemon slices, peeled cooked shrimp and sprigs of fresh dill to garnish

Using a rolling pin, firmly roll slices of bread to flatten. To prepare sauce, melt butter in a small saucepan. Stir in flour and cook 1 minute, stirring constantly. Pour in milk. Bring to a boil, stirring constantly. Reduce heat and simmer 2 minutes, stirring constantly. Remove from heat. Stir in cheese, lemon peel, chopped shrimp and parsley. Season with salt and pepper. Mix well. Spread sauce on flattened bread. Roll up, jelly-roll style. Cut each roll in 5 slices. Half-fill a deep medium-size saucepan with oil. Heat to 375F (190C) or until a cube of day-old bread browns in 40 seconds. Meanwhile, dip each roll into beaten egg and coat in bread crumbs. Fry in hot oil until golden. Drain on paper towels. Thread lemon slices and shrimp on wooden picks; push into rolls. Garnish with dill. Serve hot. Makes 20 rolls.

Angels on Horseback

6 shelled fresh oysters or 6 bottled or canned oysters, drained
2 teaspoons lemon juice
2 tablespoons finely chopped fresh parsley
1 teaspoon Worcestershire sauce
Pepper to taste
2 slices bacon
2 large slices whole-wheat bread
2 tablespoons butter, softened
Lemon peel twists to garnish

In a medium-size bowl, combine oysters, lemon juice, 1/2 tablespoon of parsley and Worcestershire sauce. Season with pepper. Mix well. Cover and refrigerate 30 minutes. Meanwhile, preheat oven to 400F (200C). On a flat surface, flatten and stretch bacon slices to twice their original length using flat side of a knife. Cut each slice into 3 pieces. Drain oysters; discard marinade. Wrap each oyster in a piece of bacon. Secure bacon with wooden picks. Place oysters on a baking sheet. Bake in preheated oven 10 to 12 minutes or until crisp. Meanwhile toast bread. Using a 2-inch plain round cutter, cut 3 rounds from each slice of toast. Stand upright to cool. Spread tops and edges of toast rounds with butter. Coat edges in remaining parsley and sprinkle remainder on top. Cool oysters slightly, then place on toast rounds. Garnish with lemon peel twists. Makes 6 pieces.

Variation: To prepare *Devils on Horseback,* fill 6 pitted prunes with a small amount of mild mango pickle relish or hot pickle relish. Wrap each prune in a piece of bacon. Secure with wooden picks. Bake as directed above. Garnish with sprigs of curly endive.

Cream Cheese Bites

4 slices pumpernickel bread
2 teaspoons dairy sour cream or
    mayonnaise
3 tablespoons very finely chopped fresh
    parsley
4 (3-oz.) packages cream cheese
1/3 cup butter, softened
1 tablespoon tomato paste
1/8 teaspoon cayenne pepper
1 to 2 teaspoons concentrated curry paste
    or 1 to 2 teaspoons curry powder plus
    1 to 2 teaspoons mayonnaise
1 garlic clove, crushed
6 seedless black grapes, cut in half
6 seedless green grapes, cut in half
Small sprigs of fresh chervil to garnish

Using a 1-1/2-inch plain round cutter, cut 6 rounds from each slice of bread. Spread edges of bread rounds lightly with sour cream and dip into parsley to coat. In a medium-size bowl, mix cream cheese and butter until soft and well combined. Put 1/2 of cream cheese mixture into another bowl. In 1 bowl, mix tomato paste and cayenne pepper into cream cheese mixture. In other bowl, mix curry paste and garlic into cream cheese mixture. In a pastry bag fitted with a large star tube, pipe tomato mixture in a swirl over 12 bread rounds. Clean bag and pipe curry mixture onto remaining bread rounds. Lightly press 6 curry rounds onto 6 tomato rounds, curry side up, and 6 tomato rounds onto 6 curry rounds, tomato side up. Place black grapes on tomato mixture and green grapes on curry mixture. Garnish with chervil. Makes 12 pieces.

Variation: Substitute white or whole-wheat toast rounds for pumpernickel bread. Coat buttered edges with poppy seeds. Garnish with walnut or pecan halves.

Lobster Rounds

6 ozs. cooked fresh or frozen lobster,
    thawed if frozen, chopped
2 small stalks celery, finely chopped
3 tablespoons mayonnaise
1/8 teaspoon cayenne pepper
Salt to taste
1/4 cup butter, softened
1 teaspoon fresh lemon juice
1 tablespoon chopped fresh parsley
6 slices pumpernickel bread
8 thin slices cucumber
8 radishes and 8 sprigs of fresh parsley
    to garnish

In a medium-size bowl, combine lobster, celery, 2 tablespoons of mayonnaise and cayenne pepper. Season with salt. Mix well. In a small bowl, mix butter, lemon juice and chopped parsley. Using a round 2-inch fluted or plain cutter, cut 4 rounds from each slice of bread. Butter 8 bread rounds on 1 side and remaining 16 on both sides. Cover 8 rounds buttered on 1 side with 1 cucumber slice each. Spread with 1/2 of lobster mixture. Top with 8 bread rounds buttered on both sides. Press together lightly. Spread with remaining lobster mixture and top with remaining bread rounds buttered on both sides. Spread tops of buttered bread rounds with remaining mayonnaise. Cut radishes in small wedge-shaped slices. Arrange in spoke-like fashion on top of each bread round. Garnish with radishes and sprigs of parsley. Makes 8 pieces.

Variation: Substitute white crabmeat or chopped shrimp for lobster.

Egg-Chive Tea Sandwiches

2 hard-cooked eggs, peeled
2 tablespoons mayonnaise
2 teaspoons chopped fresh chives
Salt and pepper to taste
1/4 cup butter, softened
2 large thin slices whole-wheat bread
2 large thin slices white bread
8 stuffed green olives and tiny sprigs of
    fresh chervil to garnish

In a medium-size bowl, mash eggs finely with a fork. Add mayonnaise and chives. Season with salt and pepper. Mix well. Butter bread. Using a 2-inch round cutter, cut 4 rounds from each slice of bread. Cover whole-wheat bread rounds with egg mixture. Using a 1/4-inch clover-leaf shaped cutter, cut shapes from center of white bread rounds; place on top of egg mixture. Press down lightly. Cut each olive in 3 thick slices. Garnish each tea sandwich with 3 olive slices and chervil. Makes 8 pieces.

Variation: Substitute watercress (green part only) for chives. Lightly flavor egg mixture with a small amount of curry paste.

Taramasalata Stars

8 thin slices whole-wheat or white bread
3 tablespoons butter, softened
2 tablespoons toasted sesame seeds
6 to 8 ozs. tarama
4 pitted black olives, cut in slivers, and
    sprigs of fresh parsley to garnish

Toast bread until light golden. Stand upright to cool. Using a 2-inch star-shaped cutter, cut 8 stars from toast. Butter stars. Sprinkle sesame seeds over buttered stars; shake off excess. In a pastry bag fitted with a large star tube, pipe a generous rosette of tarama onto each star. Garnish with olives and parsley. Makes 8 pieces.

Variation: Substitute softened cream cheese for tarama. Substitute finely chopped chives for toasted sesame seeds.

Bierwurst-Cheese Stack

1/4 cup butter, softened
2 large slices white bread, crusts removed
1 large slice whole-wheat bread, crust removed
1 carrot, grated
2 teaspoons chopped chives
1 tablespoon Thousand Island dressing
3 slices Bierwurst or bologna, rinds removed
1 medium-size tomato, thinly sliced
Salt and pepper to taste
1-1/2 ozs. red-veined Cheddar cheese, sliced
2 or 3 red leaf lettuce leaves
4 carrot curls and additional chopped chives to garnish

Butter white bread on 1 side and whole-wheat bread on both sides. In a small bowl, combine carrot, chives and 1 teaspoon of dressing. Spread carrot mixture on 1 slice of buttered white bread. Top with Bierwurst. Arrange tomato slices over Bierwurst. Sprinkle with 1 teaspoon of dressing. Season with salt and pepper. Cover with buttered whole-wheat bread. Arrange cheese slices on top. Cover with lettuce leaves. Spread remaining slice of buttered white bread with remaining dressing; place on lettuce leaves. Press together firmly. Cut diagonally in quarters. To garnish, thread 4 wooden picks with carrot curls; push into each quarter. Sprinkle with additional chopped chives. Makes 1 sandwich.

Variation: Substitute sliced salami, ham or garlic sausage for Bierwurst. Substitute blue cheese dressing, yogurt or mayonnaise for Thousand Island dressing.

Spicy Shrimp Tempters

4 ozs. peeled cooked fresh or frozen shrimp, thawed if frozen, drained, coarsely chopped
2 tablespoons Thousand Island dressing
2 teaspoons tomato paste
1 teaspoon prepared creamed horseradish
Salt and pepper to taste
3 tablespoons butter, softened
4 square slices light rye bread, crusts removed
Sprigs of fresh watercress
4 small radicchio leaves
8 peeled cooked small shrimp

In a medium-size bowl, combine shrimp, dressing, tomato paste and horseradish. Season with salt and pepper. Mix well. Butter bread. Reserve 2 sprigs of watercress. Cover 2 slices of buttered bread with remaining watercress and top with shrimp mixture. Cover with radicchio leaves. Place remaining slices of buttered bread on top. Press together firmly. Cut diagonally in quarters. Secure a small shrimp to each triangle with a wooden pick. Garnish with reserved watercress. Makes 8 pieces.

Variations: Substitute thinly sliced sesame seed Greek bread for light rye bread; do not remove crusts.

Substitute crisp green lettuce leaves for raddichio leaves.

Avocado Bites

1 tablespoon safflower oil
1 teaspoon fresh lemon juice
1/8 teaspoon sugar
1/8 teaspoon dry mustard
Salt and pepper to taste
1 small ripe avocado
1/4 cup butter, softened
2 large thin slices white bread, crusts
   removed
1 large thin slice whole-wheat bread,
   crusts removed
Radish flowers to garnish

To make dressing, in a small bowl, whisk safflower oil, lemon juice, sugar and dry mustard. Season with salt and pepper. Whisk until well combined. Cut avocado in half and remove pit. Peel avocado; cut in thin slices. Drizzle with dressing. Butter white bread on 1 side and whole-wheat bread on both sides. Arrange 1/2 of avocado slices over 1 slice of buttered white bread. Cover with buttered whole-wheat bread. Arrange remaining avocado slices over buttered whole-wheat bread. Top with remaining slices of buttered white bread. Press together firmly. Cut in quarters to form squares, then cut each square diagonally in half to form triangles. Garnish with radish flowers. Makes 8 pieces.

Variations: Add a slice of Westphalian ham, cut to fit bread, before adding avocado.

Cut sandwich in dainty shapes using heart and diamond-shaped cutters.

French Toast Fingers

1 egg
1 tablespoon milk
2 or 3 drops hot-pepper sauce
2 teaspoons tomato paste
1 small garlic clove, if desired, crushed
Salt and pepper to taste
2 slices whole-grain bread, crusts
   removed
2 tablespoons butter
1 slice processed Cheddar cheese
1 small tomato, thinly sliced
2 teaspoons chopped fresh chives

In a small bowl, beat egg, milk, hot-pepper sauce, tomato paste and garlic, if desired. Season with salt and pepper. Mix well. Soak bread in egg mixture. Melt butter in a medium-size skillet. Gently fry soaked bread until golden and crisp on both sides, turning several times. Remove from pan. While still hot, cover 1 slice of fried bread with cheese and tomato. Sprinkle with 1 teaspoon of chives. Top with remaining slice of fried bread. Press together lightly. Cut in 3 fingers. Garnish along center of fingers with remaining chives. Serve hot. Makes 1 sandwich.

Variation: To make *Sweet French Toast*, beat egg, milk, 1/4 teaspoon vanilla extract and finely grated peel of 1 small orange. Fry as directed. Sprinkle with a mixture of 1 tablespoon light brown sugar and 1/2 teaspoon ground cinnamon. Cut diagonally in quarters. Garnish with small orange twists and sliced fresh strawberries.

Salami Sandwich

1-1/2 teaspoons unsalted butter, softened
1 slice light rye bread, cut diagonally in half
2 slices green peppercorn salami or pistachio Mortadella
3 or 4 radishes, sliced
1 tablespoon French dressing
4 pitted black olives
Gherkin pickle fan and sprigs of fresh cilantro to garnish

Butter bread. Cut slices of salami in half. Form each half in a cone shape. Place cones joined-side down on buttered bread, slightly overlapping. Dip radish slices into dressing. Arrange in overlapping rows over remaining area of buttered bread. Place an olive in each salami cone. Garnish with pickle fan and cilantro. Makes 1 sandwich.

Variation: Pipe softened cream cheese into salami cones. Sprinkle with a few snipped chives.

Note: To make a pickle fan, cut 3 or 4 (1/8-inch) slices from stalk end through to pointed ends of a small gherkin pickle. Carefully open slices to form a fan.

Salmon Cocktails

4 ozs. fresh or frozen white crabmeat, thawed if frozen, finely flaked
2 tablespoons mayonnaise
1 tablespoon chopped fresh chives
Few drops Worcestershire sauce
Salt and pepper to taste
2 slices pumpernickel bread, crusts removed
3 tablespoons butter, softened
4 ozs. thinly sliced smoked salmon
Red leaf lettuce leaves
8 lemon twists and sprigs of fresh dill to garnish

In a medium-size bowl, mix crabmeat, mayonnaise, chives and Worcestershire sauce. Season with salt and pepper. Mix well. Cut each slice of bread in 4 (2-1/2" x 1-1/2")rectangles. Butter bread. Fold or cut salmon in 8 (4" x 2") rectangles. Spoon 1 tablespoon of crab filling on 1 end of salmon and roll up. Cover buttered bread with lettuce leaves. Place a salmon roll on top. Garnish with lemon twists and dill. Makes 8 pieces

Variations: Substitute toasted light rye bread for pumpernickel bread. Cover buttered bread with watercress sprigs. Substitute coarsely chopped shrimp for crabmeat.

Asparagus Rolls

8 frozen asparagus spears
8 very thin slices whole-wheat bread,
  crusts removed
1/2 cup butter, softened
1/8 teaspoon cayenne pepper
2 teaspoons fresh lemon juice
2 tablespoons finely chopped fresh
  parsley
Small radish flowers and sprigs of fresh
  Italian parsley to garnish

Cook asparagus spears according to package directions. Drain well and pat dry on paper towels. Using a rolling pin, roll each slice of bread to flatten slightly. In a small bowl, mix butter, cayenne pepper, lemon juice and chopped parsley until soft and well combined. Spread 1/2 of butter mixture on flattened bread. Trim asparagus stalks to fit across width of buttered bread. Place an asparagus spear on 1 short end of each slice of bread. Roll up tightly, jelly-roll style. Wrap each roll in plastic wrap. Refrigerate 1 hour to chill. In a pastry bag fitted with a small star tube, pipe remaining butter mixture lengthwise along each roll. Garnish with radish flowers and parsley sprigs. Serve immediately. Makes 8 rolls.

Variation: Substitute canned asparagus spears for frozen asparagus spears. Drain well and pat dry before using.

Avocado-Shrimp Cocktail Sandwich

2 tablespoons French dressing
2 ozs. peeled cooked fresh or frozen
  shrimp, thawed if frozen
1-1/2 teaspoons unsalted butter, softened
1 slice pumpernickel bread
Sprigs of fresh watercress
1/2 small ripe avocado
2 teaspoons fresh lemon juice
Salt and pepper to taste
2 tablespoon mayonnaise
Sprigs of fresh dill and lemon peel curls
  to garnish

In a small bowl, whisk dressing. Add shrimp. Stir well. Cover and refrigerate 1 hour, stirring occasionally. Drain shrimp. Butter bread. Arrange watercress on buttered bread, slightly overlapping watercress on edges of bread. Peel avocado, cut in thin slices lengthwise and dip into lemon juice. Arrange avocado slices over watercress. Season with salt and pepper. Arrange diagonal rows of shrimp over avocado slices. Using a pastry bag fitted with a small star tube, pipe mayonnaise between rows of shrimp. Garnish with dill and lemon peel. Makes 1 sandwich.

Cucumber-Mint Coolers

1/4 cucumber, peeled, thinly sliced
1/2 teaspoon salt
2 teaspoons finely chopped fresh mint
1/8 teaspoon sugar
1/4 teaspoon fresh lemon juice
3 tablespoons butter, softened
4 thin slices whole-wheat or white bread,
    crusts removed
Pepper to taste
Sprigs of fresh mint to garnish

Place cucumber slices in a sieve. Sprinkle with salt; press down with a saucer. Let drain 30 minutes. Pat cucumber slices dry on paper towels. In a small bowl, mix finely chopped mint, sugar, lemon juice and butter until soft and creamy. Butter bread. Arrange cucumber slices on 2 slices of buttered bread. Season with pepper. Cover with remaining slices of buttered bread. Press together firmly. Cut in squares or fingers. Garnish with mint. Makes 8 pieces.

Deviled Crab Treats

4 ozs. fresh or frozen white crabmeat,
    thawed if frozen
2 tablespoons mayonnaise
Few drops fresh lemon juice
Few drops hot-pepper sauce
1/4 teaspoon dry mustard
Salt and pepper to taste
3 tablespoons butter, softened
4 thin slices whole-wheat or white bread,
    crusts removed
1 or 2 crisp lettuce leaves, finely
    shredded
1 teaspoon paprika
Lemon twist and sprigs of fresh
    watercress to garnish

Flake crabmeat into a medium-size bowl. Reserve 1 teaspoon of mayonnaise. Add remaining mayonnaise, lemon juice, hot-pepper sauce and dry mustard to crabmeat. Season with salt and pepper. Mix lightly. Butter bread. Spread 2 slices of buttered bread with crabmeat mixture. Top with shredded lettuce. Cover with remaining slices of buttered bread. Press together firmly. Cut diagonally in quarters. Very lightly spread reserved mayonnaise on every other edge of each sandwich. Dip mayonnaise coated edges into paprika. Garnish with lemon twist and watercress. Makes 8 pieces.

Variations: Substitute peeled, thinly sliced cucumber for shredded lettuce.

Coat edges in finely chopped chives instead of paprika, or coat half in paprika and remainder in chives.

Peach Cream Croissants

2 croissants
2 tablespoons butter, softened
2 teaspoons fresh orange juice
2 teaspoons powdered sugar
2 ripe fresh peaches, peeled, pitted,
   thinly sliced
2/3 cup whipping cream
2 orange twists to decorate

Cut croissants at an angle 2/3 way through center, cutting from rounded side through to pointed side; do not cut through crust. In a small bowl, mix butter, 1 teaspoon of orange juice and 1 teaspoon of powdered sugar. Spread over cut sides of croissants. Arrange peaches in overlapping rows over bottom of each croissant. In a small bowl, whip cream until soft peaks form. Add remaining orange juice and powdered sugar. Whip until stiff and glossy. In a pastry bag fitted with a large star tube, pipe whipping cream mixture over peaches. Press croissant tops down lightly. Decorate with orange twists. Serve at once. Makes 2 croissants.

Variations: Substitute nectarines, strawberries, figs or kiwifruit for peaches.

Ginger Banana Cream

2 tablespoons butter, softened
2 thick slices crusty white poppy seed
   bread
2 small bananas
1/3 cup whipping cream, stiffly whipped
1 teaspoon fresh lime juice
1 or 2 pieces stem ginger in syrup,
   drained
2 teaspoons stem ginger syrup
2 lime slices and sliced pistachio nuts to
   decorate

Butter bread. In a small bowl, mash 1 banana. Fold in 2/3 of whipping cream and 1/2 teaspoon of lime juice. Spread banana mixture over buttered bread. Slice remaining banana and dip into remaining lime juice. Arrange banana slices diagonally in overlapping rows on top of banana mixture. Cut stem ginger in half, then in thin wedge-shaped slices. Arrange between sliced bananas. Top with remaining whipping cream and drizzle with stem ginger syrup. Decorate with lime slices and nuts. Serve at once. Makes 2 sandwiches.

Muesli Toppers

1/4 cup muesli
1 Red or Green Delicious apple, peeled, cored, grated
1/3 cup coarsely chopped mixed nuts
2 teaspoons fresh lemon juice
2 teaspoons honey
2 small oranges
2 thick slices raisin bread
2 tablespoons butter
1/4 cup cottage cheese, blended until smooth
8 fresh strawberries, hulled, sliced
Fresh whole strawberries and fresh sprigs of mint to garnish

In a small bowl, mix muesli, apple, nuts, lemon juice and honey. Using a sharp serrated knife, peel oranges and remove segments from skin membranes. Toast bread. Stand upright to cool. Butter toast. Top with cottage cheese. Cover with muesli mixture. Arrange rows of orange segments and sliced strawberries on top. Decorate with whole strawberries and mint. Serve immediately. Makes 2 sandwiches.

Variations: Substitute plain yogurt for cottage cheese. Substitute tropical style or other fruited muesli for muesli.

Black Cherry Delights

1 (15-oz.) can pitted black cherries, drained, juice reserved
1 tablespoon cornstarch
1 tablespoon kirsch
3 tablespoons dairy sour cream
6 medium-thick slices white bread, crusts removed
2 eggs, beaten
2 teaspoons sugar
1/2 teaspoon allspice
1/4 cup butter
Additional dairy sour cream

To prepare cherry sauce, in a small saucepan, blend reserved cherry juice, cornstarch and kirsch. Bring to a boil, stirring constantly. Reduce heat and cook 2 minutes, stirring constantly. Remove from heat. Cut cherries in half.

Spread 3 tablespoons sour cream on 3 slices of bread. Cover with cherry halves. Top with remaining slices of bread. Press firmly. In a medium-sized bowl, beat eggs, sugar and allspice. Dip sandwiches on both sides and edges into egg mixture. Heat butter in a large skillet. Fry sandwiches 5 minutes or until golden brown, turning once. Meanwhile, reheat cherry sauce. Cut fried sandwiches diagonally in quarters. Top with cherry sauce and dollops of additional sour cream. Serve at once. Makes 3 sandwiches.

Variations: Substitute 1 tablespoon orange juice for kirsch. Substitute whole-wheat bread for white bread.

Brie & Apple Slices on Rye

3 tablespoons butter, softened
2 tablespoons chopped walnuts
4 square slices light rye bread, crusts
 removed
4 (1/4-inch-thick) lengthwise slices Brie
 cheese
1/2 Green Delicious apple
1/2 Red Delicious apple
1 tablespoon fresh lemon juice
Sprigs of fresh watercress to garnish

In a small bowl, combine butter and
walnuts. Butter bread. Cut slices of
cheese in half crosswise. Arrange 2
pieces of cheese on each slice of buttered bread. Cut apples in quarters and
remove cores; do not peel. Thinly slice
apples and brush with lemon juice. Arrange overlapping alternate slices of
green and red apples over cheese. Cut
each tea sandwich diagonally in half.
Garnish with watercress. Makes 8
pieces.

Melon & Ham Fingers

2 slices pumpernickel bread, crusts
 removed
1/3 cup butter, softened
1 teaspoon fresh lemon juice
1-1/2 teaspoons tomato paste
1/4 small ripe honeydew melon, seeded
3 thin slices prosciutto, cut in half
 lengthwise
Sprigs of fresh dill to garnish

Cut each slice of bread in 3 (3" x 1 1/2")
fingers. In a small bowl, mix butter and
lemon juice. Spread a small amount on
bread fingers. Blend remaining butter
mixture with tomato paste. Mix well. In
a pastry bag fitted with a small plain
tube, pipe thin diagonal parallel lines of
butter mixture over buttered bread.
Refrigerate to chill. Using a small
melon baller, scoop 12 balls from
melon. Pat dry on paper towels. Thread
a melon ball onto a wooden pick.
Gather a half slice of ham and thread
onto wooden pick. Add another melon
ball to wooden pick. Arrange at a slight
angle over buttered bread. Garnish
with dill. Makes 6 pieces.

Tropical Shortcake

2 (3-oz.) packages cream cheese, softened
Finely grated peel 1 small lemon
3 tablespoons whipping cream
1 shortcake, cut in half
2 kiwifruit, peeled, thinly sliced
Toasted blanched almonds and 2 maraschino cherries, cut in half,
   to decorate

In a small bowl, mix cream cheese, lemon peel and whipping cream. Toast shortcake halves until light golden. Stand upright to cool. Spread each half with 2/3 of cream cheese mixture. Reserve 2 slices of kiwifruit. Overlap remaining slices of kiwifruit on top of cream cheese mixture. In a pastry bag fitted with a large star tube, pipe remaining cream cheese mixture in a rosette in center of each shortcake. Cut reserved slices of kiwifruit from 1 side through to center. Twist and place on top of cream cheese mixture. Decorate with almonds and maraschino cherry halves. Makes 2 shortcakes.

Sweety Pies

8 large medium-thick slices white bread,
   crusts removed
1/4 cup butter, melted
1/2 cup mincemeat
Finely grated peel 1 orange
1 egg, beaten
Julienne strips orange peel and whipped
   cream to decorate

Preheat oven to 375F (190C). Using a rolling pin, roll each slice of bread firmly to flatten. Brush both sides of flattened bread with butter. Press 4 sides of buttered bread into 4 (4-inch) fluted pans, pressing bread well into flutes. Using flat side of a knife, press firmly around edges of bread to cut. In a small bowl, mix mincemeat and orange peel. Fill each bread-lined pan with 2 tablespoons of mincemeat mixture; level surfaces. Using a small star-shaped cutter, cut a star from center of each remaining slice of buttered bread. Place slice of buttered bread over mincemeat. Using flat side of a knife, press firmly around edges of bread to cut. Lift edges of bread. Brush generously with beaten egg, then press edges firmly together to seal. Place pans on a baking sheet. Bake in preheated oven 20 to 25 minutes or until golden. Cool slightly. Meanwhile, bring a small saucepan of water to a boil. Add strips of orange peel. Cook 3 minutes. Drain, plunge into cold water and pat dry on paper towels. To decorate, in a pastry bag fitted with a plain tube, pipe whipped cream to one side of stars. Sprinkle with orange peel. Serve warm. Makes 4 pies.

Index